1970

—the military use of herbicides in South Vietnam.

THE WITHERING RAIN

Also by Thomas Whiteside

THE
WITHERING RAIN
America's Herbicidal Folly

THOMAS WHITESIDE

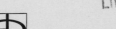

E. P. Dutton & Co., Inc., New York 1971

TO

William Shawn

Contents

Introduction

I would like to preface this book with some notes on my own involvement with the subject of the potential hazards of the chemical 2,4,5-T and with American defoliation and herbicidal programs here and in Southeast Asia. As a citizen, I had followed, for several years, and with a sense of increasing dismay, the great expansion in Vietnam of American military defoliation and crop-destruction programs there. The subject had not been covered, except in a very sketchy fashion, by the press or by television, but it seemed clear to me from what I had read that whatever military gains the Defense Department considered it might make through its defoliation and herbicidal operations in Vietnam, very great privation was being visited on the civilian population exposed to these operations. My concern over the consequences of the use of 2,4,5-T deepened when, in mid-October, 1969, I learned—not from an American newspaper but through an item in the London *Sunday Times*—of the existence and principal findings of an unpublished government-sponsored study by Bionetics Research Laboratories of Bethesda, Maryland, concerning the fetus-deforming activity of

2,4,5-T upon pregnant mice and rats in controlled laboratory experiments.

I was then in the middle of a fairly long writing project, but I was sufficiently disturbed about the implications of this information to begin doing some work, as a reporter, on the 2,4,5-T situation. At first, I thought that I might write a short comment in the Talk of the Town section of *The New Yorker* on the potential hazards to humans that seemed to be connected with the use of 2,4,5-T, but after my investigations had been under way for some time, it became clear to me that what was involved was far more than the single issue of the use of one potentially dangerous substance, and it also became clear that the research that I would have to do would be very extensive.

What was manifestly involved in the subject I was looking into was an astonishing—really, a shocking—laxity in proper standards for the manufacture and use of a broad range of highly complex chemicals put out by big chemical companies and showered into the environment and brought into close contact with human beings without adequate prior testing in the laboratory for potential adverse effects on man, on animals, and on aquatic and plant life. I found 2,4,5-T itself to be part of a family of chemicals known as polychlorinated phenolic compounds that were seemingly almost ubiquitous and that were being used in such common products as paper, paints, varnishes, timber, soaps, hair shampoos, and laundry starches, as well as in the most widely used of all herbicides, 2,4-D. Yet these chemicals had never been adequately studied, either singly or as a class, for their potential harmfulness to humans, in spite of available evidence that many of the chemicals or their contaminants or breakdown products were capable of producing frightening toxic effects. I was dismayed to discover what seemed to me to be a thoroughgoing failure on the part of government regulatory agencies to set or enforce proper standards of safety for a huge number of what are officially classified as "economic poisons"—a failure uncorrected, I might observe, eight years after the publication of Rachel Carson's prescient *Silent Spring,* which had warned of the serious hazards to the environment and to man himself of the massive and heedless use of the chlorinated hydrocarbon pesticides such as DDT.

I also found a thoroughgoing failure on the part of government officials of various agencies to keep one another properly informed of vital scientific data concerning potentially dangerous chemicals. As for their keeping the public properly informed of the facts about these widely used chemicals, I found that government officials were not only failing to do this but, in the case of the potential dangers of 2,4,5-T, which was being so widely used in defoliation operations in Vietnam, information about these potential hazards simply had to be dragged out of them, and that this unforthright attitude reached into the office of the President's own science advisers. As a layman venturing into the world of science to write what now loomed as a long and complex article, I discovered that my predisposition toward a rather indiscriminate respect for scientists required a certain tempering. I found some scientists connected with the government to be both disdainful and at the same time suspicious of lay inquiries into their own professional world, and unwilling to cooperate with a serious journalistic investigation; some of them seemed to throw the mantle of science over themselves and their work as some militarist might figuratively wrap himself in the flag. I was hardly surprised to find officials of the Dow Chemical Company, one of the largest manufacturers of 2,4,5-T, uncommunicative. But I was taken aback to encounter plain antagonism from several scientists connected with the government when I raised with them what I thought were reasonable questions about the way in which information on the studies of the teratogenic, or fetus-deforming, activity of 2,4,5-T in experimental animals had been handled. They intimated that such matters were beyond the understanding of laymen and comprehensible only to professional biologists.

I found this kind of attitude disappointing in people who I had supposed were devoted to the search for scientific truth. I formed the suspicion that this professional grandiosity was in part something very like a cover for timidity—a reluctance to discuss even a *prima facie* case against potentially dangerous compounds for fear of a whipping by professional critics at the next scientific convention. In such an aura, scientists and government officials who were certainly well equipped to understand the potential dangers of 2,4,5-T somehow withheld information from the scientific community and the public on the teratogenic nature of this chemical for three years, during which time the United States military sprayed, according to my calculations, probably close to 15,000 tons of 2,4,5-T on the Vietnamese countryside and on Vietnamese civilians and their food and water supplies. When I approached a responsible official of Bionetics Laboratories, which had actually carried out the study on 2,4,5-T under a government contract, he wasn't at all eager to talk about the results of the study. He said that because of the nature of the issues involved, the study was a "sensitive" one. He virtually waved away any implications for humans arising out of the findings of the study, even though these findings had been that 2,4,5-T exerted clearly teratogenic effects on experimental mice and rats. To make sure that I understood him clearly, I asked the Bionetics official, "If your wife and family were living in the country and an airplane sprayed a thousand gallons of 2,4,5-T over the area where they lived, at the spray rate used in Vietnam, would you be concerned for their safety?"

"Let me answer this way," he said. "If cyclamates were still available, my family would still be drinking them."

I persisted. "Would you be concerned?" I asked.

"I wouldn't be concerned about it," he answered. Then, after a pause, he added, "Of course if the dose was repeated for weeks or a month that might be a different matter."

Yet what we were talking about was a spray rate of 2,4,5-T that, at least as laid down in Vietnam, could result in a pregnant Vietnamese woman's ingesting close to an equivalent amount of 2,4,5-T that, in experimental rats, deformed one out of three of the rats' unborn offspring.

Even well after the information indicating the teratogenicity of 2,4,5-T had been forced into the open, I encountered considerable reluctance by government officials frankly to face what seemed to me to be the gravity of the issues involved. A scientist at the White House, one of the officials responsible for compiling scientific advice for the President, told me at one point, "If we have to spend money on research on 2,4,5-T, my hunch is that spending it on research into the relationship between 2,4,5-T and humans isn't the best place to put the money."

When I telephoned one independent scientist, a well-known specialist in the science of teratology, who lives in the Midwest, and attempted to obtain some enlightenment concerning the probable significance of the Bionetics findings on 2,4,5-T in relation to those on other known teratogens, including thalidomide, I encountered a depressingly familiar note of scientific grandiosity: the scientist informed me, "To be blunt, I don't think you know what you're talking about." When I told him that I stood ready to have my understanding improved, he refused to discuss the subject over the telephone, and suggested that I write him a letter of inquiry, which, however, he would not guarantee to answer. I did not write the letter. I mention this incident because I believe it illustrates the difficulties a layman may encounter when he attempts to penetrate the mysteries of a certain kind of scientific outlook. The teratologist involved was certainly a highly qualified expert in his field, and I was an inquiring journalist to whom the scientific questions raised by the unfavorable reports on 2,4,5-T were certainly most formidable to comprehend. Yet this question remains in my mind—why was it left to a journalist to pull together, with great effort, information from all sorts of quarters on the potential hazards of 2,4,5-T and its indiscriminate use for years on civilian populations without adequate tests ever having been made for its safety? Where had that eminent teratologist been during all that time—what had he been doing about the potential hazards of herbicides?

Fortunately I did encounter, during my researches into the uses of 2,4,5-T and related chemicals, other scientists who extended to me most patient and helpful cooperation. These scientists include the biologists Professor Arthur W. Galston of

Yale, Professor Egbert W. Pfeiffer of the University of Montana, Professor Arthur H. Westing of Windham College, Professor Matthew S. Meselson of Harvard, and Dr. Samuel S. Epstein of the Children's Cancer Research Foundation in Boston, and the toxicologists Dr. Joseph McLaughlin and Dr. Jacqueline Verrett of the Food and Drug Administration.

When I began to realize the scope of the investigations I was undertaking, I had, of course, to consider whether I should not go to Vietnam to look into the effects of defoliation operations there. After thinking the matter over, I decided not to go to Vietnam, on the ground that what needed to be investigated most were the government and industry standards—or lack of them—that had made the defoliation and herbicidal programs in Vietnam possible in the first place, and that had permitted these programs to grow to their present huge size. And I concluded that these problems could most profitably be explored in this country by an examination of the circumstances through which potentially dangerous chemicals could be approved for such widespread use without adequate testing.

The article that I wrote on the basis of these researches appeared in the February 7, 1970, issue of *The New Yorker,* and when it did I assumed with considerable relief that its publication would mark an end to my efforts to bring the potential dangers of 2,4,5-T to public attention, and that the newspapers and television people, realizing the importance of this issue of public safety, would take up where I had left off on the question of 2,4,5-T and other defoliants and herbicides. I hoped that the force of informed public opinion would then cause the government to cease the unrestricted use of these chemicals until they had been shown beyond reasonable doubt not to be potentially harmful to human life. Unfortunately, the newspapers, weekly news magazines, and television networks almost unanimously ignored the issue, and I found myself in a strange position. I was confident that the facts about the potential hazards of 2,4,5-T and other polychlorinated phenolic compounds would eventually sink in and result in proper standards being established and enforced for the use of these chemicals, but it appeared that in the meantime their continued use would expose millions of people in this country and in Southeast Asia to the potential hazards of damage to the unborn. Up to then, I had taken the attitude that somehow, once a writer brings out facts that need to be brought out, he's done his job and he can move on to his next project. But the unpleasant fact now confronted me that just *writing* wasn't enough, and that unless I took some sort of personal action the impact of this journalistic investigation would be quickly dissipated by other issues coming to public attention. In an attempt to prevent this from happening, I telephoned various friends at newspapers, news magazines, and broadcasting networks. The result of these communications was approximately zero. I was particularly distressed that *The New York Times,* with its staff of experienced science reporters, was taking no real action to investigate and report in detail on the potential dangers of 2,4,5-T and other defoliants and herbicides——even though the *Times* was aware of and had reported the rather equivocal announcement on October 29, 1969, by Dr. Lee DuBridge, the President's science adviser, promising "a coordinated series of actions" by government agencies to restrict the uses of 2,4,5-T. (I later was gently informed, through a responsible and experienced member of the *Times* editorial staff, that the *Times* made a practice of staying away, where it possibly could, from such issues if the paper hadn't actually uncovered and developed the story itself. It seemed to me that, if this were true, it reflected a serious problem in the editorial direction of the *Times,* particularly since it is without real competition as a newspaper of record.)

In my frustration at this failure of the media to pursue what I considered so important a subject, I turned to other means, and put in a couple of telephone calls to people I knew in Washington, to let them know that the information I had, and that a number of very competent biologists had, was that the data concerning the teratogenic properties of 2,4,5-T and related compounds were very disturbing, and that some sort of official investigation deserved to be made into the standards that made possible the widespread use of these chemicals without adequate testing. This time, there was a positive response, and on February 12, Senator Philip A. Hart, chairman of the Senate Subcommittee (of the Committee on Commerce) on Energy, Natural Resources, and the Environment, announced that the subcommittee would hold a series of official hearings on "the effects of 2,4,5-T and related herbicides on man and the environment."

By this time, faced with a continued failure of the press and television to take up the herbicide issue in a serious way, I had decided to continue my investigation and reporting on the subject, and the result of this work was a series of further amplifying articles in the form of letters to the editors of *The New Yorker,* which were published in the magazine.

The Congressional hearings were held on April 7 and 15, and again on June 17 and 18, and, largely owing to the inability of the Administration to sustain its position before this committee of inquiry that 2,4,5-T posed no potential hazards to human health, Dr. Jesse L. Steinfeld, the Surgeon General of the United States, announced, on April 15, a number of measures that he said would limit the use of 2,4,5-T in this country. These included the immediate suspension by the Department of Agriculture of registrations for the use of liquid formulations around the home and of all formulations used for killing vegetation around lakes, ponds, and irrigation ditches. The Surgeon General also announced that the Department of Agriculture would cancel its registrations of nonliquid formulations of 2,4,5-T around the home and on food crops in this country. On the same day, Deputy Secretary of Defense David Packard announced the immediate suspension of the use of 2,4,5-T in Vietnam. This was a considerable step forward, but as I have attempted to show in this book, the announced measures sounded far more sweeping in scope than they really were, so that the overall use of 2,4,5-T, in this country anyway, was not substantially affected by these orders.

As this is written, the use of potentially dangerous polychlorinated phenolic compounds, of which 2,4,5-T is but one, continues on a very wide scale. In view of the fact that once a pesticidal compound has been registered with the Department of Agriculture and put into widespread use, the commercial momentum generated by its continued manufacture and sale is such that when doubts arise as to its safety the burden of proof concerning these suspicions in effect shifts from the chemical companies to the government, which is simply not organized to establish this proof, one wonders—especially in the face of the open lack of enthusiasm on the part of government officials to change the customary commercial order of things—who *is* protecting the public. There is no doubt that there is a most pressing need for a thorough overhaul of the existing pesticide-control legislation and that the terms of its prohibitions and regulatory standards should be made so clear and unequivocal that the regulatory agencies, concerned citizens, and federal courts alike know just what Congress intends and requires of the regulatory agencies on behalf of the public. I also believe that a good case can be made for the creation of an organization independent of industrial or direct governmental control to carry out systematic environmental studies of potentially dangerous chemicals and to serve as a kind of distant early warning system concerning the environmental effects of industrial poisons. My journalistic experience with governmental bungling over 2,4,5-T convinces me that only limited reliance can be placed on federal agencies to carry out and act upon this kind of research. After all, it was not as a scientist of the Department of Agriculture that Rachel Carson spoke out on the dangers of pesticides that were revealed in *Silent Spring.* But it *was* the Department of Agriculture that permitted and indeed encouraged the very chemical abuses and long-range hazards that made that work such a powerful indictment of the behavior of industry and the government regulatory bureaucracy alike.

In the meantime, it seems to me that so far as the polychlorinated phenolic compounds that are dealt with in this book are concerned, it is only through unceasing vigilance and pressure on Congress, industry, and the regulatory agencies by people who are determined to reverse the escalation of the already widespread potential hazards to the living and to the unborn

from highly complex yet inadequately tested chemical substances and formulations that the production, sale, and use of
these chemicals can be effectively outlawed or put under rigor-
ous control here. A start has now been made toward proper
protection of the public from the hazards of 2,4,5-T and related
compounds, but the constant political pressures exerted by the
chemical industry, the reluctance of the federal regulatory
bureaucracy to interfere with rich markets, and the self-per-
petuating nature of chemical-warfare programs within the military establishment together form a force that requires great
effort to counter effectively. Characteristically, an attempt on the
floor of the Senate in August, 1970, by Senators Charles
Goodell of New York and Gaylord Nelson of Wisconsin to
amend the military-procurement bill for 1971 by denying ap-
propriations for herbicidal-warfare programs in Southeast Asia
was defeated by a vote of 66 to 22. Prior to this, President Nixon,
in submitting the text of the Geneva Protocol, which is aimed at
outlawing chemical and biological warfare, to the Senate for
ratification, made it clear in advance that his Administration did
not choose to consider that herbicidal warfare was covered in
the prohibitions of the Protocol. However, not all interested
parties have yet been heard from on this question. The Administration has been heard from, the Pentagon has been heard from,
some senators have been heard from, but an informed public
has yet to make its strength felt. Again, I believe that it is only
through strong and insistent public representations that defoliation and crop destruction programs by the military will be
formally renounced by the United States and outlawed inter-
nationally as instruments of chemical and biological warfare
covered by the terms of the Geneva Protocol. But I do believe
that these representations of the people will be made, and that
in spite of all the resistance they *can* be made to prevail.

November, 1970

THE WITHERING RAIN

1

Defoliation in Vietnam

Late in 1961, the United States Military Advisory Group in Vietnam began, as a minor test operation, the defoliation, by aerial spraying, of trees along the sides of roads and canals east of Saigon. The purpose of the operation was to increase visibility and thus safeguard against ambushes of allied troops and make more vulnerable any Vietcong who might be concealed under cover of the dense foliage. The number of acres sprayed does not appear to have been publicly recorded, but the test was adjudged a success militarily. In January, 1962, following a formal announcement by South Vietnamese and American officials that a program of such spraying was to be put into effect, and that it was intended "to improve the country's economy by permitting freer communication as well as to facilitate the Vietnamese Army's task of keeping these avenues free of Vietcong harassments," military defoliation operations really got under way. According to an article that month in *The New York Times,* "a high South Vietnamese official" announced that a seventy-mile stretch of road between Saigon and the coast was sprayed "to remove foliage hiding Communist guerrillas." The

South Vietnamese spokesman also announced that defoliant chemicals would be sprayed on Vietcong plantations of manioc and sweet potatoes in the Highlands. The program was gathering momentum. It was doing so in spite of certain private misgivings among American officials, particularly in the State Department, who feared, first, that the operations might open the United States to charges of engaging in chemical and biological warfare, and, second, that they were not all that militarily effective. Roger Hilsman, now a professor of government at Columbia University, and then Director of Intelligence and Research for the State Department, reported, after a trip to Vietnam, that defoliation operations "had political disadvantages" and, furthermore, that they were of questionable military value, particularly in accomplishing their supposed purpose of reducing cover for ambushes. Hilsman later recalled in his book, *To Move a Nation,* his visit to Vietnam, in March, 1962: "I had flown down a stretch of road that had been used for a test and found that the results were not very impressive. . . . Later, the senior Australian military representative in Saigon, Colonel Serong, also pointed out that defoliation actually aided the ambushers—if the vegetation was close to the road those who were ambushed could take cover quickly; when it was removed the guerrillas had a better field of fire." According to Hilsman, "The National Security Council spent tense sessions debating the matter."

Nonetheless, the Joint Chiefs of Staff and their chairman, General Maxwell Taylor, agreed that chemical defoliation was a useful military weapon. In 1962, the American military "treated" 4,940 acres of the Vietnamese countryside with herbicides. In 1963, the area sprayed increased fivefold, to a total of 24,700 acres. In 1964, the defoliated area was more than tripled. In 1965, the 1964 figure was doubled, increasing to 155,610 acres. In 1966, the sprayed area was again increased fivefold, to 741,247 acres, and in 1967 it was doubled once again over the previous year, to 1,486,446 acres. Thus, the areas defoliated in Vietnam had increased approximately three hundredfold in five years, but now adverse opinion among scientists and other people who were concerned about the effects of defoliation on the Vietnamese ecology at last began to have a braking effect on the program. In 1968, 1,267,110 acres were sprayed, and in 1969 perhaps a million acres. Since 1962, the defoliation operations have covered almost five million acres, an area equivalent to about twelve per cent of the entire territory of South Vietnam, and about the size of the state of Massachusetts. Between 1962 and 1967, the deliberate destruction of plots of rice, manioc, beans, and other foodstuffs through herbicidal spraying—the word "deliberate" is used here to exclude the many reported instances of accidental spraying of Vietnamese plots—increased three hundredfold, from an estimated 741 acres to 221,312 acres, and by the end of 1969 the Vietnamese crop-growing area that since 1962 had been sprayed with herbicides totaled at least half a million acres. By then, in many areas the original purpose of the defoliation had been all but forgotten. The military had discovered that a more effective way of keeping roadsides clear was to bulldoze them. But by the time of that discovery defoliation had settled in as a general policy and taken on a life of its own—mainly justified on the ground that it made enemy infiltration from the North much more difficult by removing vegetation that concealed jungle roads and trails.

During all the time since the program began in 1961, no American military or civilian official has ever publicly characterized it as an operation of either chemical or biological warfare, although there can be no doubt that it is an operation of chemical warfare in that it involves the aerial spraying of chemical substances with the aim of gaining a military advantage, and that it is an operation of biological warfare in that it is aimed at a deliberate disruption of the biological conditions prevailing in a given area. Such distinctions simply do not appear in official United States statements or documents; they were long ago shrouded under heavy verbal cover. Thus, a State Department report, made public in March, 1966, saying that about twenty thousand acres of crops in South Vietnam had been destroyed by defoliation to deny food to guerrillas, described the areas involved as "remote and thinly populated," and gave a firm assurance that the materials sprayed on the crops were of a mild and transient potency: "The herbicides used are nontoxic and not dangerous to man or animal life. The land is not affected for future use."

However comforting the statements issued by our government during seven full years of herbicidal operations in Vietnam, the fact is that the major development of defoliant chemicals (whose existence had been known in the thirties) and other herbicidal agents came about in military programs for biological warfare. The direction of this work was set during the Second World War, when Professor E. J. Kraus, who then headed the botany department of the University of Chicago, brought certain scientific possibilities to the attention of a committee that had been set up by Henry L. Stimson, the Secretary of War, under the National Research Council, to provide the military with advice on various aspects of biological warfare. Kraus, referring to the existence of hormone-like substances that experimentation had shown would kill certain plants or disrupt their growth, suggested to the committee in 1941 that it might be interested in "the toxic properties of growth-regulating substances for the destruction of crops or the limitation of crop production." Military research on herbicides thereupon got under way, principally at Camp (later Fort) Detrick, Maryland, the Army center for biological-warfare research. According to George Merck, a chemist, who headed Stimson's biological-warfare advisory committee, "Only the rapid ending of the war prevented field trials in an active theater of synthetic agents that would, without injury to human or animal life, affect the growing crops and make them useless."

After the war, many of the herbicidal materials that had been developed and tested for biological-warfare use were marketed for civilian purposes and used by farmers and homeowners for killing weeds and controlling brush. The most powerful of the herbicides were the two chemicals 2,4-dichlorophenoxyacetic acid, generally known as 2,4-D, and 2,4,5-trichlorophenoxyacetic acid, known as 2,4,5-T. The direct toxicity levels of these chemicals as they affected experimental animals, and, by scientific estimates, men, appeared then to be low (although these estimates have later been challenged), and the United States Department of Agriculture, the Food and Drug Administration, and the Fish and Wildlife Service all sanctioned the widespread sale and use of both. The chemicals were also reported to be short-lived in soil after their application. 2,4-D was the bigger seller of the two, partly because it was cheaper, and suburbanites commonly used mixtures containing 2,4-D on their lawns to control dandelions and other weeds. Commercially, 2,4-D and 2,4,5-T were used to clear railroad rights-of-way and power-line routes, and, in cattle country, to get rid of woody brush, 2,4,5-T being favored for the last, because it was considered to have a more effective herbicidal action on woody plants. Very often, however, the two chemicals were used in combination. Between 1945 and 1963, the production of herbicides jumped from 917,000 pounds to about 150,000,000 pounds in this country; since 1963, their use has risen 271 per cent—more than double the rate of increase in the use of pesticides, though pesticides are still far more extensively used. By 1960, an area equivalent to more than three per cent of the entire United States was being sprayed each year with herbicides.

Considering the rapidly growing civilian use of these products, it is perhaps not surprising that the defoliation operations in Vietnam escaped any significant comment in the press, and that the American public remained unaware of the extent to which these uses had their origin in planning for chemical and biological warfare. Nevertheless, between 1941 and the present, testing and experimentation in the use of 2,4-D, 2,4,5-T, and other herbicides as military weapons were going forward very actively at Fort Detrick. While homeowners were using herbicidal mixtures to keep their lawns free of weeds, the military were screening some twelve hundred compounds for their usefulness in biological-warfare operations. The most promising of these compounds were test-sprayed on tropical vegetation in Puerto Rico and Thailand, and by the time full-scale defoliation operations got under way in Vietnam the U.S. military had settled on the use of four herbicidal spray materials there. These went under the names Agent Orange, Agent Purple, Agent White, and Agent Blue—designations derived from color-coded strips girdling the shipping drums of each type of material. Of these materials, Agent Orange, the most widely used as a general defoliant, consists of a fifty-fifty mixture of n butyl esters of 2,4-D and 2,4,5-T. Agent Purple, which is interchangeable with Agent Orange, consists of the same substances with slight molecular variations. Agent White, which is used mostly for forest defoliation, is a combination of 2,4-D and picloram, produced by the Dow Chemical Company. Unlike 2,4-D or 2,4,5-T, which, after application, is said to be decomposable by microorganisms in soil over a period of weeks or months (one field test of 2,4,5-T in this country showed that significant quantities persisted in soil for ninety-three days after application), picloram—whose use the Department of Agriculture has not authorized in the cultivation of any American crop—is one of the most persistent herbicides known. Dr. Arthur W. Galston, professor of biology at Yale, has described picloram as "a herbicidal analog of DDT," and an article in a Dow Chemical Company publication called "Down to Earth" reported that in field trials of picloram in various California soils between eighty and ninety-six and a half per cent of the substance remained in the soils four hundred and sixty-seven days after application. (The rate at which picloram decomposes in tropical soils may, however, be higher.) Agent Blue consists of a solution of cacodylic acid, a substance that contains fifty-four per cent arsenic, and it is used in Vietnam to destroy rice crops. According to the authoritative *Merck Index,* a source book on chemicals, this material is "poisonous." It can be used on agricultural crops in this country only under certain restrictions imposed by the Department of Agriculture. It is being used herbicidally on Vietnamese rice fields at seven and a half times the concentration permitted for weed-killing purposes in this country, and so far in Vietnam something like five thousand tons is estimated to have been sprayed on paddies and vegetable fields.

Defoliation operations in Vietnam are carried out by a special flight of the 12th Air Commando Squadron of the United States Air Force, from a base at Bien Hoa, just outside Saigon, with specially equipped C-123 cargo planes. Each of these aircraft has been fitted out with tanks capable of holding a thousand gallons. On defoliation missions, the herbicide carried in these tanks is sprayed from an altitude of around a hundred and fifty feet, under pressure, from thirty-six nozzles on the wings and tail of the plane, and usually several spray planes work in formation, laying down broad blankets of spray. The normal crew of a military herbicidal-spray plane consists of a pilot, a copilot, and a technician, who sits in the tail area and operates a console regulating the spray. The equipment is calibrated to spray a thousand gallons of herbicidal mixture at a rate that works out, when all goes well, to about three gallons per acre. Spraying a thousand-gallon tankload takes five minutes. In an emergency, the tank can be emptied in thirty seconds— a fact that has particular significance because of what has recently been learned about the nature of at least one of the herbicidal substances.

The official code name for the program is Operation Hades, but a more friendly code name, Operation Ranch Hand, is commonly used. In similar fashion, military public-relations men refer to the herbicidal spraying of crops supposedly grown for Vietcong use in Vietnam, when they refer to it at all, as a "food-denial program." By contrast, an American biologist who is less than enthusiastic about the effort has called it, in its current phase, "escalation to a program of starvation of the population in the affected area." Dr. Jean Mayer, the Harvard professor who now is President Nixon's special adviser on nutrition, contended in an article in *Science and Citizen* in 1967 that the ultimate target of herbicidal operations against rice and other crops in Vietnam was "the weakest element of the civilian population"—that is, women, children, and the elderly—because in the sprayed areas "Vietcong soldiers may . . . be expected to get the fighter's share of whatever food there is." He pointed out that malnutrition is endemic in many parts of Southeast Asia but that in wartime South Vietnam, where diseases associated with malnutrition, such as beriberi, anemia, kwashiorkor (the disease that has decimated the Biafran population), and tuberculosis, are particularly widespread, "there can be no doubt that if the [crop-destruction] program is continued, [the] problems will grow."

Whether a particular mission involves defoliation or crop destruction, American military spokesmen insist that a mission never takes place without careful consideration of all the factors involved, including the welfare of friendly inhabitants and the safety of American personnel. (There can be little doubt that defoliation missions are extremely hazardous to the members of the planes' crews, for the planes are required to fly very low and only slightly above stalling speed, and they are often targets of automatic-weapons fire from the ground.) The process of setting up targets and approving specific herbicidal operations is theoretically subject to elaborate review through two parallel chains of command: one chain consisting of South Vietnamese district and province chiefs—who can themselves initiate such missions—and South Vietnamese Army commanders at various levels; the other a United States chain, consisting of a district adviser, a sector adviser, a divisional senior adviser, a corps senior adviser, the United States Military Assistance Command in South Vietnam, and the American Embassy in Saigon, ending up with the American ambassador himself. Positive justification of the military advantage likely to be gained from each operation is theoretically required, and applications without such positive justification are theoretically disapproved. However, according to one of a series of articles by Elizabeth Pond that appeared toward the end of 1967 in the *Christian Science Monitor:*

> In practice, [American] corps advisers find it very difficult to turn down defoliation requests from province level because they simply do not have sufficient specific knowledge to call a proposed operation into question. And with the momentum of six years' use of defoliants, the practice, in the words of one source, has long since been "set in cement."
>
> The real burden of proof has long since shifted from the positive one of justifying an operation by its [military] gains to

the negative one of denying an operation because of [specific] drawbacks. There is thus a great deal of pressure, especially above province level, to approve recommendations sent up from below as a matter of course.

Miss Pond reported that American military sources in Saigon were "enthusiastic" about the defoliation program, and that American commanders and spotter-plane pilots were "clamoring for more of the same." She was given firm assurances as to the mild nature of the chemicals used in the spray operations:

> The defoliants used, according to the military spokesman contacted, are the same herbicides . . . as those used commercially over some four million acres in the United States. In the strengths used in Vietnam they are not at all harmful to humans or animals, the spokesman pointed out, and in illustration of this he dabbed onto his tongue a bit of liquid from one of . . . three bottles sitting on his desk.

As the apparently inexorable advance of defoliation operations in South Vietnam continued, a number of scientists in the United States began to protest the military use of herbicides, contending that Vietnam was being used, in effect, as a proving ground for chemical and biological warfare. Early in 1966, a group of twenty-nine scientists, under the leadership of Dr. John Edsall, a professor of biochemistry at Harvard, appealed to President Johnson to prohibit the use of defoliants and crop-destroying herbicides, and called the use of these substances in Vietnam "barbarous because they are indiscriminate." In the late summer of 1966, this protest was followed by a letter of petition to President Johnson from twenty-two scientists, including seven Nobel laureates. The petition pointed out that the "large-scale use of anticrop and 'non-lethal' antipersonnel chemical weapons in Vietnam" constituted "a dangerous precedent" in chemical and biological warfare, and it asked the President to order it stopped. Before the end of that year, Dr. Edsall and Dr. Matthew S. Meselson, a Harvard professor of biology, obtained the signatures of five thousand scientists to cosponsor the petition. Despite these protests, the area covered by defoliation operations in Vietnam in 1967 was double that covered in 1966, and the acreage of crops destroyed was nearly doubled.

These figures relate only to areas that were sprayed intentionally. There is no known way of spraying an area with herbicides from the air in a really accurate manner, because the material used is so highly volatile, especially under tropical conditions, that even light wind drift can cause extensive damage to foliage and crops outside the deliberately sprayed area. Crops are so sensitive to the herbicidal spray that it can cause damage to fields and gardens as much as fifteen miles away from the target zone. Particularly severe accidental damage is reported, from time to time, to so-called "friendly" crops in the III Corps area, which all but surrounds Saigon and extends in a rough square from the coastline to the Cambodian border. Most of the spraying in III Corps is now done in War Zones C and D, which are classified as free fire zones, where, as one American official has put it, "everything that moves in Zones C and D is considered Charlie." A press dispatch from Saigon in 1967 quoted another American official as saying that every Vietnamese farmer in that corps area knew of the defoliation program and disapproved of it. Dr. Galston, the Yale biologist, who is one of the most persistent critics of American policy concerning herbicidal operations in Vietnam, recently said in an interview, "We know that most of the truck crops grown along roads, canals, and trails and formerly brought into Saigon have been essentially abandoned because of the deliberate or inadvertent falling of these defoliant sprays; many crops in the Saigon area are simply not being harvested." He also cited reports that in some instances in which the inhabitants of Vietnamese villages have been suspected of being Vietcong sympathizers the destruction of food crops has brought about complete abandonment of the villages. In 1966, herbicidal operations caused extensive inadvertent damage, through wind drift, to a very large rubber plantation northwest of Saigon owned by the Michelin rubber interests. As the result of claims made for this damage, the South Vietnamese authorities paid the corporate owners, through the American military, nearly a million dollars. The extent of the known inadvertent damage to crops in Vietnam can be inferred from the South Vietnamese budget—in reality, the American military budget—for settling such claims. In 1967, the budget for this compensation was $3,600,-000. This sum, however, probably reflects only the barest emergency claims of the people affected.

According to Representative Richard D. McCarthy, a Democrat from upstate New York who has been a strong critic of the program, the policy of allowing applications for defoliation operations to flow, usually without question, from the level of the South Vietnamese provincial or district chiefs has meant that these local functionaries would order repeated sprayings of areas that they had not visited in months, or even years. The thought that a Vietnamese district chief can initiate such wholesale spraying, in effect without much likelihood of serious hindrance by American military advisers, is a disquieting one to a number of biologists. Something that disquiets many of them even more is what they believe the long-range effects of nine years of defoliation operations will be on the ecology of South Vietnam. Dr. Galston, testifying recently before a congressional subcommittee on chemical and biological warfare, made these observations:

> It has already been well documented that some kinds of plant associations subject to spray, especially by Agent Orange, containing 2,4-D and 2,4,5-T, have been irreversibly damaged. I refer specifically to the mangrove associations that line the estuaries, especially around the Saigon River. Up to a hundred thousand acres of these mangroves have been sprayed. . . . Some [mangrove areas] had been sprayed as early as 1961 and have shown no substantial signs of recovery. . . . Ecologists have known for a long time that the mangroves lining estuaries furnish one of the most important ecological niches for the completion of the life cycle of certain shellfish and migratory fish. If these plant communities are not in a healthy state, secondary effects on the whole interlocked web of organisms are bound to occur. . . . In the years ahead the Vietnamese, who do not have overabundant sources of proteins anyhow, are probably going to suffer dietarily because of the deprivation of food in the form of fish and shellfish.

Damage to the soil is another possible consequence of extensive defoliation. . . . We know that the soil is not a dead, inert mass but, rather, that it is a vibrant, living community. . . . If you knock the leaves off of trees once, twice, or three times . . . you change the quality of the soil. . . . Certain tropical soils—and it has been estimated that in Vietnam up to fifty per cent of all the soils fall into this category—are laterizable; that is, they may be irreversibly converted to rock as a result of the deprivation of organic matter. . . . If . . . you deprive trees of leaves and photosynthesis stops, organic matter in the soil declines and laterization, the making of brick, may occur on a very extensive scale. I would emphasize that this brick is irreversibly hardened; it can't be made back into soil. . . .

Another ecological consequence is the invasion of an area by undesirable plants. One of the main plants that invade an area that has been defoliated is bamboo. Bamboo is one of the most difficult of all plants to destroy once it becomes established where you don't want it. It is not amenable to killing by herbicides. Frequently it has to be burned over, and this causes tremendous dislocations to agriculture.

Dr. Fred H. Tschirley, assistant chief of the Crops Protection Research Branch of the Department of Agriculture, who made a month's visit to Vietnam in the spring of 1968 in behalf of the State Department to report on the ecological effects of herbicidal operations there, does not agree with Dr. Galston's view that laterization of the soil is a serious probability. However, he reported to the State Department that in the Rung Sat area, southeast of Saigon, where about a hundred thousand acres of mangrove trees had been sprayed with defoliant, each single application of Agent Orange had killed ninety to a hundred per cent of the mangroves touched by the spray, and he estimated that the regeneration of the mangroves in this area would take another twenty years, at least. Dr. Tschirley agrees with Dr. Galston that a biological danger attending the defoliation of mangroves is an invasion of virtually ineradicable bamboo.

A fairly well-documented example not only of the ecological consequences of defoliation operations but also of their disruptive effects on human life was provided last year by a rubber-plantation area in Kompong Cham Province, Cambodia, which lies just across the border from Vietnam's Tay Ninh Province. On June 2, 1969, the Cambodian government, in an angry diplomatic note to the United States government, charged the United States with major defoliation damage to rubber plantations, and also to farm and garden crops in the province, through herbicidal operations deliberately conducted on Cambodian soil. It demanded compensation of eight and a half million dollars for destruction or serious damage to 24,000 acres of trees and crops. After some delay, the State Department conceded that the alleged damage might be connected with "accidental drift" of spray over the border from herbicidal operations in Tay Ninh Province. The Defense Department flatly denied that the Cambodian areas had been deliberately sprayed. Late in June, the State Department sent a team of four American scientists to Cambodia, and they confirmed the extent of the area of damage that the Cambodians had claimed. They found that although some evidence of spray drift across the Vietnamese border existed, the extent and severity of damage in the area worst affected were such that "it is highly unlikely that this quantity could have drifted over from the Tay Ninh defoliation operations." Their report added, "The evidence we have seen, though circumstantial, suggests strongly that damage was caused by direct overflight." A second report on herbicidal damage to the area was made after an unofficial party of American biologists, including Professor E. W. Pfeiffer, of the University of Montana, and Professor Arthur H. Westing, of Windham College, Vermont, visited Cambodia last December at the invitation of the Cambodian government. They found that about a third of all the rubber trees currently in production in Cambodia had been damaged, and this had happened in an area that normally had the highest latex yield per acre of any in the world. A high proportion of two varieties of rubber trees in the area had died as a result of the damage, and Dr. Westing estimated that the damage to the latex-producing capacity of some varieties might persist for twenty years. Between May and November of last year, latex production in the affected plantations fell off by an average of between thirty-five and forty per cent. According to a report by the two scientists, "A large variety of garden crops were devastated in the seemingly endless number of small villages scattered throughout the affected area. Virtually all of the . . . local inhabitants . . . depend for their well-being upon their own local produce. These people saw their crops . . . literally wither before their eyes." The Cambodian claim is still pending.

Until the end of last year, the criticism by biologists of the dangers involved in the use of herbicides centered on their use in what were increasingly construed as biological-warfare operations, and on the disruptive effects of these chemicals upon civilian populations and upon the ecology of the regions in which they were used. Last year, however, certain biologists began to raise serious questions on another score—possible direct hazards to life from 2,4,5-T. On October 29, as a result of these questions, a statement was publicly issued by Dr. Lee DuBridge, President Nixon's science adviser. In summary, the statement said that because a laboratory study of mice and rats that had been given relatively high oral doses of 2,4,5-T in early stages of pregnancy "showed a higher than expected number of deformities" in the offspring, the government would, as a precautionary measure, undertake a series of coordinated actions to restrict the use of 2,4,5-T in both domestic civilian applications and military herbicidal operations. The DuBridge statement identified the laboratory study as having been made by an organization called the Bionetics Research Laboratories in Bethesda, Maryland, but gave no details of either the findings or the data on which they were based. This absence of specific information turned out to be characteristic of what has been made available to the public concerning this particular research project. From the beginning, it seems, there was an extraordinary reluctance to discuss details of the purported ill effects of 2,4,5-T on animals. Six weeks after the publication of the DuBridge statement, a journalist who was attempting to obtain a copy of the full report made by Bionetics and to discuss its details with some of the government officials concerned encountered hard going. At the Bionetics Laboratories, an official said that he couldn't talk about the study, because "we're under wraps to the National Institutes of Health"—the government agency that commissioned the study. Then, having been asked what the specific doses of 2,4,5-T were that were said to have increased birth defects in the fetuses of experimental animals, the Bionetics official cut off discussion by saying, "You're asking sophisticated questions that as a layman you don't have the equipment to understand the answers to." At the National Institutes of Health, an official who was asked for details of or a copy of the study on 2,4,5-T replied, "The position I'm in is that I have been requested not to distribute this information." He did say, however, that a continuing evaluation of the study was under way at the National Institute of Environmental Health Sciences, at Research Triangle Park, North Carolina. A telephone call to an officer of this organization brought a response whose tone varied from wariness to downright hostility and made it clear that the official had no intention of discussing details or results of the study with the press.

The Bionetics study on 2,4,5-T was part of a series carried out under contract to the National Cancer Institute, which is an arm of the National Institutes of Health, to investigate more than two hundred compounds, most of them pesticides, in order to determine whether they induced cancer-causing changes, fetus-deforming changes, or mutation-causing changes in experimental animals. The contract was a large one, involving more than two and a half million dollars' worth of research, and its primary purpose was to screen out suspicious-looking substances for further study. The first visible fruits of the Bionetics research were presented in March of last year before a convention of the American Association for the Advancement of Science, in the form of a study of possible carcinogenic properties of fifty-three compounds; the findings on 2,4,5-T were that it did not appear to cause carcinogenic changes in the animals studied.

By the time the report on the carcinogenic properties of the substances was presented, the results of another part of the

Bionetics studies, concerning the teratogenic, or fetus-deforming, properties of the substances, were being compiled, but these results were not immediately made available to biologists outside the government. The data remained—somewhat frustratingly, in the view of some scientists who had been most curious about the effects of herbicides—out of sight, and a number of attempts by biologists who had heard about the teratological study of 2,4,5-T to get at its findings appear to have been thwarted by the authorities involved. Upon being asked to account for the apparent delay in making this information available to biologists, an official of the National Institute of Environmental Health Sciences (another branch of the National Institutes of Health) has declared, with some heat, that the results of the study itself and of a statistical summary of the findings prepared by the Institute were in fact passed on as they were completed to the Commission on Pesticides and Their Relationship to Environmental Health, a scientific group appointed by Secretary of Health, Education, and Welfare Robert Finch and known—after its chairman, Dr. E. M. Mrak, of the University of California—as the Mrak Commission. Dr. Samuel S. Epstein, chief of the Laboratories of Environmental Toxicology and Carcinogenesis at the Children's Cancer Research Foundation in Boston, who was cochairman of the Mrak Commission panel considering the teratogenic potential of pesticides, tells a different story on the availability of the Bionetics study. He says that he first heard about it in February. At a meeting of his panel in August, he asked for a copy of the report. Ten days later, the panel was told that the National Institute of Environmental Health Sciences would be willing to provide a statistical summary but that the group could not have access to the full report on which the summary was based. Dr. Epstein says that the panel eventually got the full report on September 24 "by pulling teeth."

Actually, as far back as February, officials at the National Cancer Institute had known, on the basis of a preliminary written outline from Bionetics, the findings of the Bionetics scientists on the fetus-deforming role of 2,4,5-T. Dr. Richard Bates, the officer of the National Institutes of Health who was in charge of coordinating the Bionetics project, has said that during the same month this information was put into the hands of officials of the Food and Drug Administration, the Department of Agriculture, and the Department of Defense. "We had a meeting with a couple of scientists from Fort Detrick, and we informed them of what we had learned," Dr. Bates said recently. "I don't know whether they were the right people for us to see. We didn't hear from them again until after the Du-Bridge announcement at the White House. Then they called up and asked for a copy of the Bionetics report."

At the Department of Agriculture, which Dr. Bates said had been informed in February of the preliminary Bionetics findings, Dr. Tschirley, one of the officials most intimately concerned with the permissible uses of herbicidal compounds, says that he first heard about the report on 2,4,5-T through the DuBridge announcement. At the Food and Drug Administration, where appropriate officials had been informed in February of the teratogenic potential of 2,4,5-T, no new action was taken to safeguard the public against 2,4,5-T in foodstuffs. In fact, it appears that no action at all was taken by the Food and Drug Administration on the matter during the whole of last year. The explanation that F.D.A. officials have offered for this inaction is that they were under instructions to leave the whole question alone at least until December, because the matter was under definitive study by the Mrak Commission—the very group whose members, as it turns out, had such extraordinary difficulty in obtaining the Bionetics data. The Food Toxicology Branch of the F.D.A. did not have access to the full Bionetics report on 2,4,5-T until after Dr. DuBridge issued his statement, at the end of October.

Thus, after the first word went to various agencies about the fetus-deforming potential of 2,4,5-T, and warning lights could have flashed on in every branch of the government and in the headquarters of every company manufacturing or handling it, literally almost nothing was done by the officials charged with protecting the public from exposure to dangerous or potentially dangerous materials—by the officials in the F.D.A., in the Department of Agriculture, and in the Department of Defense. It is conceivable that the Bionetics findings might still be hidden from the public if they had not been pried loose in midsummer through the activities of a group of young law students. The students were members of a team put together by the consumer-protection activist Ralph Nader—and often referred to as Nader's Raiders—to explore the labyrinthine workings of the Food and Drug Administration. In the course of their investigations, one of the law students, a young woman named Anita Johnson, happened to see a copy of the preliminary report on the Bionetics findings that had been passed on to the F.D.A. in February, and its observations seemed quite disturbing to her. Miss Johnson wrote a report to Nader, and in September she showed a copy of the report to a friend who was a biology student at Harvard. In early October, Miss Johnson's friend, in a conversation with Professor Matthew Meselson, mentioned Miss Johnson's report on the preliminary Bionetics findings. This was the first that Dr. Meselson had heard of the existence of the Bionetics study. A few days previously, he had received a call from a scientist friend of his asking whether Dr. Meselson had heard of certain stories, originating with South Vietnamese journalists and other South Vietnamese, of an unusual incidence of birth defects in South Vietnam, which were alleged to be connected with defoliation operations there.

A few days later, after his friend sent him further information, Dr. Meselson decided to obtain a copy of the Bionetics report, and he called up an acquaintance in a government agency and asked for it. He was told that the report was "confidential and classified," and inaccessible to outsiders. Actually, in addition to the preliminary report there were now in existence the full Bionetics report and a statistical summary prepared by the National Institute of Environmental Health Sciences, and, by nagging various Washington friends, Dr. Meselson obtained bootlegged copies of the two latest reports. What he read seemed to him to have such serious implications that he got in touch with acquaintances in the White House and also with someone in the Army to alert them to the problems of 2,4,5-T, in the hope that some new restrictions would be placed on its use. According to Dr. Meselson, the White House people apparently didn't know until that moment that the reports on the adverse effects of 2,4,5-T even existed. (Around that time, according to a member of Nader's Raiders, "a tremendous lid was put on this thing" within government agencies, and on the subject of the Bionetics work and 2,4,5-T "people in government whom we'd been talking to freely for years just shut up and wouldn't say a word.") While Dr. Meselson awaited word on the matter, a colleague of his informed the press about the findings of the Bionetics report. Very shortly thereafter, Dr. DuBridge made his public announcement of the proposed restrictions on the use of 2,4,5-T.

In certain respects, the DuBridge announcement is a curious document. In its approach to the facts about 2,4,5-T that were set forth in the Bionetics report, it reflects considerable sensitivity to the political and international issues that lie behind the widespread use of this powerful herbicide for civilian and military purposes, and the words in which it describes the reasons for restricting its use appear to have been very carefully chosen:

> The actions to control the use of the chemical were taken as a result of findings from a laboratory study conducted by Bionetics Research Laboratories which indicated that offspring of mice and rats given relatively large oral doses of the herbicide during early stages of pregnancy showed a higher than expected number of deformities.
>
> Although it seems improbable that any person could receive harmful amounts of this chemical from any of the existing uses of 2,4,5-T, and while the relationships of these effects in laboratory animals to effects in man are not entirely clear at this time, the actions taken will assure safety of the public while further evidence is being sought.

These actions, according to the statement, included decisions that the Department of Agriculture would cancel manufacturers' registrations of 2,4,5-T for use on food crops, effective at the beginning of 1970, "unless by that time the Food and Drug

Administration has found a basis for establishing a safe legal tolerance in and on foods," and that the Departments of Agriculture and the Interior, in their own programs, would stop the use of 2,4,5-T in populated areas and in all other areas where residues of the substance could reach man. As for military uses of 2,4,5-T, the statement said, "The chemical is effective in defoliating trees and shrubs and its use in South Vietnam has resulted in reducing greatly the number of ambushes, thus saving lives." However, the statement continued, "the Department of Defense will [henceforth] restrict the use of 2,4,5-T to areas remote from the population."

All this sounds eminently fair and sensible, but whether it represents a candid exposition of the facts about 2,4,5-T and the Bionetics report is debatable. The White House statement that the Bionetics findings "indicated that offspring of mice and rats given relatively large oral doses of the herbicide during early stages of pregnancy showed a higher than expected number of deformities" is, in the words of one eminent biologist who has studied the Bionetics data, "an understatement." He went on to say that "if the effects on experimental animals are applicable to people it's a very sad and serious situation." The actual Bionetics report described 2,4,5-T as producing "sufficiently prominent effects of seriously hazardous nature" in controlled experiments with pregnant mice to lead the authors "to categorize [it] as *probably dangerous.*" The report also found 2,4-D "potentially dangerous but needing further study." As for 2,4,5-T, the report noted that, with the exception of very small subcutaneous dosages, "all dosages, routes, and strains resulted in increased incidence of abnormal fetuses" after its administration. The abnormalities in the fetuses included lack of eyes, faulty eyes, cystic kidneys, cleft palates, and enlarged livers. The Bionetics report went on to report on further experimental applications of 2,4,5-T to another species:

> Because of the potential importance of the findings in mice, an additional study was carried out in rats of the Sprague-Dawley strain. Using dosages of 21.5 and 46.4 mg/kg [that is, dosages scaled to represent 21.5 and 46.4 milligrams of 2,4,5-T

per kilogram of the experimental animal's body weight] suspended in 50 per cent honey and given by the oral route on the
6th through 15th days of gestation, we observed excessive fetal
mortality (almost 80 per cent) and a high incidence of abnormalities in the survivors. When the beginning of administration was delayed until the 10th day, fetal mortality was
somewhat less but still quite high even when dosage was reduced to 4.6 mg/kg. The incidence of abnormal fetuses was
threefold that in controls even with the smallest dosage and
shortest period used. . . .

It seems inescapable that 2,4,5-T is teratogenic in this strain
of rats when given orally at the dosage schedules used here.

Considering the fetus-deforming effects of the *lowest* oral
dosage of 2,4,5-T used in the Bionetics work on rats—to say
nothing of the excessive fetal mortality—the White House
statement that "relatively large oral doses of the herbicide . . .
showed a higher than expected number of deformities" is
hardly an accurate description of the results of the study. In
fact, the statistical tables presented as part of the Bionetics
report showed that at the lowest oral dosage of 2,4,5-T given
to pregnant rats between the tenth and fifteenth days of gestation thirty-nine per cent of the fetuses produced were abnormal,
or three times the figure for control animals. At what could
without much question be described as "relatively large oral
doses" of the herbicide—dosages of 21.5 and 46.4 milligrams
per kilogram of body weight of rats, for example—the percentage of abnormal fetuses was ninety and a hundred per cent,
respectively, or a good bit higher than one would be likely to
deduce from the phrase "a higher than expected number of
deformities." The assertion that "it seems improbable that any
person could receive harmful amounts of this chemical from any
of the existing uses of 2,4,5-T" also appears to be worth
examining, for this is precisely what many biologists are most
worried about in relation to 2,4,5-T and allied substances.

It seems fair, before going further, to quote a cautionary
note in the DuBridge statement: "The study involved relatively
small numbers of laboratory rats and mice. More extensive
studies are needed and will be undertaken. At best it is difficult

to extrapolate results obtained with laboratory animals to man
—sensitivity to a given compound may be different in man than
in animal species. . . ." It would be difficult to get a biologist
to disagree with these seemingly sound generalities. However,
the first part of the statement does imply, at least to a layman,
that the number of experimental animals used in the Bionetics
study had been considerably smaller than the numbers used to
test commercial compounds other than 2,4,5-T before they are
approved by agencies such as the Food and Drug Administration and the Department of Agriculture. In this connection, the
curious layman could reasonably begin with the recommendations, in 1963, of the President's Science Advisory Committee
on the use of pesticides, which proposed that companies putting
out pesticides should be required from then on to demonstrate
the safety of their products by means of toxicity studies on two
generations of at least two warm-blooded mammalian species.
Subsequently, the F.D.A. set up new testing requirements, based
on these recommendations, for companies producing pesticides.
However, according to Dr. Joseph McLaughlin, of the Food
Toxicology Branch of the F.D.A., the organization actually
requires applicants for permission to sell pesticides to present
the results of tests on only *one* species (usually, in practice,
the rat). According to Dr. McLaughlin, the average number
of experimental animals used in studies of pesticides is between
eighty and a hundred and sixty, including animals used as
controls but excluding litters produced. The Bionetics study
of 2,4,5-T used both mice and rats, and their total number was,
in fact, greater, not less, than this average. Including controls
but excluding litters, the total number of animals used in the
2,4,5-T studies was 225. Analysis of the results by the National
Institute of Environmental Health Sciences found them statistically "significant," and this is the real purpose of such a study:
it is meant to act as a coarse screen to shake out of the data the
larger lumps of bad news. Such a study is usually incapable of
shaking out anything smaller; another kind of study is needed
to do that.

Thus, the DuBridge statement seems to give rise to this

question: If the Bionetics study, based on the effects of 2,4,5-T on 225 experimental animals of two species, appears to be less than conclusive, on the ground that "the study involved relatively small numbers of laboratory rats and mice," what is one to think of the adequacy of the tests that the manufacturers of pesticides make? If, as the DuBridge statement says, "at best it is difficult to extrapolate results obtained with laboratory animals to man," what is one to say of the protection that the government affords the consumer when the results of tests of pesticidal substances on perhaps 120 rats are officially extrapolated to justify the use of the substances by a population of two hundred million people—not to mention one to two million unborn babies being carried in their mothers' wombs?

The very coarseness of the screen used in all these tests— that is, the relatively small number of animals involved—means that the bad news that shows up in the data has to be taken with particular seriousness, because lesser effects tend not to be demonstrable at all. The inadequacy of the scale on which animal tests with, for instance, pesticides are currently being made in this country to gain F.D.A. approval is further indicated by the fact that a fetus-deforming effect that might show up if a thousand test animals were used is almost never picked up, since the studies are not conducted on that scale; yet if the material being tested turned out to have the same effect, quantitatively, on human beings, this would mean that it would cause between three and four thousand malformed babies to be produced each year. The teratogenic effects of 2,4,5-T on experimental animals used by the Bionetics people, however, were not on the order of one in a thousand. Even in the case of the lowest oral dose given rats, they were on the order of one in three.

Again, it is fair to say that what is applicable to rats in such tests may not be applicable to human beings. But it is also fair to say that studies involving rats are conducted not for the welfare of the rat kingdom but for the ultimate protection of human beings. In the opinion of Dr. Epstein, the fact that the 2,4,5-T used in the Bionetics study produced teratogenic effects in *both* mice and rats underlines the seriousness of the study's implications. In the opinion of Dr. McLaughlin, this is even further underlined by another circumstance—that the rat, as a test animal, tends to be relatively resistant to teratogenic effects of chemicals. For example, in the late nineteen-fifties, when thalidomide, that disastrously teratogenic compound, was being tested on rats in oral dosages ranging from low to very high, no discernible fetus-deforming effects were produced. And Dr. McLaughlin says that as far as thalidomide tests on rabbits were concerned, "You could give thalidomide to rabbits in oral doses at between fifty and two hundred times the comparable human level to show any comparable teratogenic effects." In babies born to women who took thalidomide, whether in small or large dosages and whether in single or multiple dosages, between the sixth and seventh weeks of pregnancy, the rate of deformation was estimated to be one in ten.

Because of the relatively coarse testing screen through which compounds like pesticides—and food additives as well—are sifted before they are approved for general or specialized use in this country, the Food and Drug Administration theoretically maintains a policy of stipulating, as a safety factor, that the maximum amount of such a substance allowable in the human diet range from one two-thousandth to one one-hundredth of the highest dosage level of the substance that produces no harmful effects in experimental animals. (In the case of pesticides, the World Health Organization takes a more conservative view, considering one two-thousandth of the "no-effect" level in animal studies to be a reasonable safety level for human exposure.) According to the standards of safety established by F.D.A. policy, then, no human being anywhere should ever have been exposed to 2,4,5-T, because in the Bionetics study of rats *every* dosage level produced deformed fetuses. A "no-effect" level was never achieved.

To make a reasonable guess about the general safety of 2,4,5-T for human beings, as the material has been used up to now, the most appropriate population area to observe is probably not the relatively healthy and well-fed United States, where human beings are perhaps better equipped to withstand the assault of toxic substances, but South Vietnam, where great numbers of civilians are half-starved, ravaged by disease, and racked by the innumerable horrors of war. In considering any potentially harmful effects of 2,4,5-T on human beings in Vietnam, some attempt has to be made to estimate the amount of 2,4,5-T to which people, and particularly pregnant women, may have been exposed as a result of the repeated defoliation operations. To do so, a comparison of known rates of application of 2,4,5-T in the United States and in Vietnam is in order. In this country, according to Dr. Tschirley, the average recommended application of 2,4,5-T in aerial spraying for woody-plant control is between three-quarters of a pound and a pound per acre. There are about five manufacturers of 2,4,5-T in this country, of which the Dow Chemical Company is one of the biggest. One of Dow Chemical's best-sellers in the 2,4,5-T line is Esteron 245 Concentrate, and the cautionary notes that a drum of Esteron bears on its label are hardly reassuring to anyone lulled by prior allegations that 2,4,5-T is a substance of low toxicity:

CAUTION—
MAY CAUSE SKIN IRRITATION
Avoid Contact with Eyes, Skin, and Clothing
Keep out of the reach of children

Under the word "WARNING" are a number of instructions concerning safe use of the material, and these include, presumably for good reason, the following admonition:

Do not contaminate irrigation ditches or water used for domestic purposes.

Then comes a "NOTICE":

Seller makes no warranty of any kind, express or implied, concerning the use of this product. Buyer assumes all risk of use or handling, whether in accordance with directions or not.

The concentration of Esteron recommended—subject to all these warnings, cautions, and disclaimers—for aerial spraying in the United States varies with the type of vegetation to be sprayed, but probably a fair average would be three-quarters to one pound acid equivalent of the raw 2,4,5-T per acre. In Vietnam, however, the concentration of 2,4,5-T for each acre sprayed has been far higher. In Agent Orange, the concentrations of 2,4,5-T have averaged *thirteen times* the recommended concentrations used in the United States. The principal route through which quantities of 2,4,5-T might be expected to enter the human system in Vietnam is through drinking water, and in the areas sprayed most drinking water comes either from rainwater cisterns fed from house roofs or from very shallow wells. It has been calculated that, taking into account the average amount of 2,4,5-T in Agent Orange sprayed per acre in Vietnam by the military, and assuming a one-inch rainfall (which is quite common in South Vietnam) after a spraying, a forty-kilo (about eighty-eight-pound) Vietnamese woman drinking two liters (about 1.8 quarts) of contaminated water a day could very well be absorbing into her system 120 milligrams, or about one two-hundred-and-fiftieth of an ounce, of 2,4,5-T a day; that is, a daily oral dosage of three milligrams of 2,4,5-T per kilo of body weight. Thus, if a Vietnamese woman who was exposed to Agent Orange was pregnant, she might very well be absorbing into her system a percentage of 2,4,5-T only slightly less than the percentage that deformed one out of every three fetuses of the pregnant experimental rats. To pursue further the question of exposure of Vietnamese to 2,4,5-T concentrations in relation to concentrations officially considered safe for Americans, an advisory subcommittee to the Secretary of the Interior, in setting up guidelines for maximum safe contamination of surface water by pesticides and allied substances some time ago, recommended a concentration of one-tenth of a milligram of 2,4,5-T in one liter of drinking water as the maximum safe concentration. Thus, a pregnant Vietnamese woman who ingested 120 milligrams of 2,4,5-T in two liters of water a day would be exposed to 2,4,5-T at six hundred times the concentration officially considered safe for Americans.

Moreover, the level of exposure of Vietnamese people in sprayed areas is not necessarily limited to the concentrations shown in Dr. Meselson's calculations. Sometimes the level may be far higher. Dr. Pfeiffer, the University of Montana biologist, says that when difficulties arise with the spray planes or the spray apparatus, or when other accidents occur, an entire thousand-gallon load of herbicidal agent containing 2,4,5-T may be dumped in one area by means of the thirty-second emergency-dumping procedure. Dr. Pfeiffer has recalled going along as an observer on a United States defoliation mission last March, over the Plain of Reeds area of Vietnam, near the Cambodian border, during which the technician at the spray controls was unable to get the apparatus to work, and thereupon dumped his whole load. "This rained down a dose of 2,4,5-T that must have been fantastically concentrated," Dr. Pfeiffer has said. "It was released on a very watery spot that looked like headwaters draining into the Mekong River, which hundreds of thousands of people use." In another instance, he has recalled, a pilot going over the area of the supposedly "friendly" Catholic refugee village of Ho Nai, near Bien Hoa, had serious engine trouble and dumped his whole spray load of herbicide on or near the village. In such instances, the concentration of 2,4,5-T dumped upon an inhabited area in Vietnam probably averaged about 130 times the concentration recommended by 2,4,5-T manufacturers as both effective and safe for use in the United States.

Theoretically, the dangers inherent in the use of 2,4,5-T should have been removed by means of the steps promised in the White House announcement last October. A quick reading of the statement by Dr. DuBridge (who is also the executive secretary of the President's Environmental Quality Council) certainly seemed to convey the impression that from that day onward there would be a change in Department of Defense policy on the use of 2,4,5-T in Vietnam, just as there would be a change in the policies of the Departments of Agriculture and the Interior on the domestic use of 2,4,5-T. But did the White

House mean what it certainly seemed to be saying about the future military use of 2,4,5-T in Vietnam? The White House statement was issued on October 29. On October 30, the Pentagon announced that no change would be made in the policy governing the military use of 2,4,5-T in South Vietnam, because—so the Washington *Post* reported on October 31— "the Defense Department feels its present policy conforms to the new Presidential directive." The *Post* article went on:

> A Pentagon spokesman's explanation of the policy, read at a morning press briefing, differed markedly from the written version given reporters later.
>
> When the written statement was distributed, reporters were told not to use the spokesman's [previous] comment that the defoliant . . . is used against enemy "training and regroupment centers."
>
> The statement was expunged after a reporter asked how use against such centers conformed to the Defense Department's stated policy of prohibiting its use in "populated areas."

But the statement wasn't so easily expunged. A short time later, it was made again, in essence, by Rear Admiral William E. Lemos, of the Policy Plans and National Security Council Affairs Office of the Department of Defense, in testimony before a subcommittee of the House Foreign Affairs Committee, the only difference being that the phrase "training and regroupment centers" became "enemy base camps." And in testifying that the military was mounting herbicidal operations on alleged enemy base camps Rear Admiral Lemos said:

> We know . . . that the enemy will move from areas that have been sprayed. Therefore, enemy base camps or unit headquarters are sprayed in order to make him move to avoid exposing himself to aerial observation.

If one adds to the words "enemy base camps" the expunged words "training and regroupment centers"—centers that are unlikely to operate without an accompanying civilian population —what the Defense Department seems actually to be indicating is that the "areas remote from the population" against which the United States is conducting military herbicidal operations are "remote from the population" at least in part *because* of these operations.

As for the Bionetics findings on the teratogenic effects of 2,4,5-T on experimental animals, the Department of Defense indicated that it put little stock in the dangers suggested by the report. A reporter for the *Yale Daily News* who telephoned the Pentagon during the first week in December to inquire about the Defense Department's attitude toward its use of 2,4,5-T in the light of the Bionetics report was assured that "there is no cause for alarm about defoliants." A week or so later, he received a letter from the Directorate for Defense Information at the Pentagon which described the Bionetics results as based on "evidence that 2,4,5-T, when fed in large amounts to highly inbred and susceptible mice and rats, gave a higher incidence of birth defects than was normal for these animals." After reading this letter, the *Yale Daily News* reporter again telephoned the Pentagon, and asked, "Does [the Department of Defense] think defoliants could be affecting embryo growth in any way in Vietnam?" The Pentagon spokesman said, "No." And that was that. The experimental animals were highly susceptible; the civilian Vietnamese population, which even under "normal" circumstances is the victim of a statistically incalculable but clearly very high abortion and infant-mortality rate, was not.

Nearly a month after Dr. DuBridge's statement, another was issued, this one by the President himself, on United States policy on chemical and biological warfare. The President, noting that "biological weapons have massive, unpredictable, and potentially uncontrollable consequences" that might "impair the health of future generations," announced it as his decision that thenceforward "the United States shall renounce the use of lethal biological agents and weapons, and all other methods of biological warfare." Later, a White House spokesman, in answer to questions by reporters whether this included the use of herbicidal, defoliant, or crop-killing chemicals in Vietnam, made it clear that the new policy did not encompass herbicides.

Since the President's statement did specifically renounce "all other methods of biological warfare," the reasonable assumption is that the United States government does not consider herbicidal, defoliant, and crop-killing operations against military and civilian populations to be part of biological warfare. The question therefore remains: What does the United States government consider biological warfare to consist of? The best place to look for an authoritative definition is a work known as the Joint Chiefs of Staff Dictionary, an official publication that governs proper word usage within the military establishment. In the current edition of the Joint Chiefs of Staff Dictionary, "biological warfare" is defined as the "employment of living organisms, toxic biological products, and plant-growth regulators to produce death or casualties in man, animals, or plants or defense against such action." But the term "plant-growth regulators" is nowhere defined in the Joint Chiefs of Staff Dictionary, and since a certain technical distinction might be made (by weed-control scientists, for example) between plant-growth regulators and defoliants, the question of whether the Joint Chiefs consider military defoliation operations part of biological warfare is left unclear. As for "defoliant agents," the Dictionary defines such an agent only as "a chemical which causes trees, shrubs, and other plants to shed their leaves prematurely." All this is hardly a surprise to anyone familiar with the fast semantic legerdemain involved in all official statements on biological warfare, in which defoliation has the bafflingly evanescent half-existence of a pea under a shell.

To find that pea in the official literature is not easy. But it is reasonable to assume that if the Department of Defense were to concede officially that "defoliant agents" were in the same category as "plant-growth regulators" that "produce death . . . in plants," it would thereby also be conceding that it is in fact engaging in the biological warfare that President Nixon has renounced. And such a concession seems to have been run to earth in the current edition of a Department of the Army publication entitled *Manual on Use of Herbicides for Military*

Purposes, in which "antiplant agents" are defined as "chemical agents which possess a high offensive potential for destroying or seriously limiting the production of food and defoliating vegetation," and goes on, "These compounds include herbicides that kill or inhibit the growth of plants; plant-growth regulators that either regulate or inhibit plant growth, sometimes causing plant death. . . ." The admission that the Department of Defense is indeed engaging, through its defoliation and herbicidal operations in Vietnam, in biological warfare, as this is defined by the Joint Chiefs and as it has been formally renounced by the President, seems inescapable.

Since the DuBridge statement, allegations, apparently originating in part with the Dow Chemical Company, have been made to the effect that the 2,4,5-T used in the Bionetics study was unrepresentative of the 2,4,5-T generally produced in this country, in that it contained comparatively large amounts of a certain contaminant, which, according to the Dow people, is ordinarily present in 2,4,5-T only in trace quantities. Accordingly, it has been suggested that the real cause of the teratogenic effects of the 2,4,5-T used in the Bionetics study may not have been the 2,4,5-T itself but, rather, the contaminant in the sample used. The chemical name of the contaminant thus suspected by the Dow people is 2,3,7,8-tetrachlorodibenzo-*p*-dioxin, often referred to simply as dioxin. The 2,4,5-T used by Bionetics was obtained in 1965 from the Diamond Alkali Company, now known as the Diamond-Shamrock Company and no longer in the business of manufacturing 2,4,5-T. It appears that the presence of a dioxin contaminant in the process of manufacturing 2,4,5-T is a constant problem among all manufacturers. In the mid-sixties, Dow was obliged to close down its 2,4,5-T plant in Midland, Michigan, for several months and partly rebuild it because of what Dow people variously described as "a problem" and "an accident." The problem—or accident—was that workers exposed to the dioxin contaminant during the process of manufacture came down with an acute skin irritation known as chloracne. The Dow people, who speak with considerable pride of their toxicological work ("We estab-

lished our toxicology lab the year Ralph Nader was born," a
Dow public-relations man said recently, showing, at any rate,
that Dow is keenly aware of Nader and his career), say that
the chloracne problem has long since been cleared up, and that
the current level of the dioxin contaminant in Dow's 2,4,5-T is
less than one part per million, as opposed to the dioxin level in
the 2,4,5-T used in the Bionetics study, which is alleged to
have been between fifteen and thirty parts per million. A
scientist at the DuBridge office, which has become a coordinating agency for information having to do with the 2,4,5-T
question, says that the 2,4,5-T used by Bionetics was "probably
representative" of 2,4,5-T being used in this country—and
presumably in Vietnam—at the time it was obtained but that
considerably less of the contaminant is present in the 2,4,5-T
now being produced. Evidently, the degree of dioxin contamination present in 2,4,5-T varies from manufacturer to manufacturer. What degree of contamination, high or low, was present
in the quantities of 2,4,5-T shipped to South Vietnam at various
times this spokesman didn't seem to know.

The point about the dioxin contamination of 2,4,5-T is an
extremely important one, because if the suspicions of the Dow
people are correct and the cause of the fetus deformities cited
in the Bionetics study is not the 2,4,5-T but the dioxin contaminant, then this contaminant may be among the most
teratogenically powerful agents ever known. Dr. McLaughlin
has calculated that if the dioxin present in the Bionetics 2,4,5-T
was indeed responsible for the teratogenic effects on the experimental animals, it looks as though the contaminant would have
to be at least ten thousand times more teratogenically active in
rats than thalidomide was found to be in rabbits. Furthermore,
it raises alarming questions about the prevalence of the dioxin
material in our environment. It appears that under high heat
the dioxin material can be produced in a whole class of
chemical substances known as trichlorophenols and pentachlorophenols. These substances include components of certain
fatty acids used in detergents and in animal feed.

As a consequence of studies that have been made of the

deaths of millions of young chicks in this country after the chicks had eaten certain kinds of chicken feed, government scientists are now seriously speculating on the possibility that the deaths were at the end of a chain that began with the spraying of corn crops with 2,4,5-T. The hypothesis is that residues of dioxin present in the 2,4,5-T remained in the harvested corn and were concentrated into certain by-products that were then sold to manufacturers of chicken feed, and that the dioxin became absorbed into the systems of the young chicks. One particularly disquieting sign of the potential of the dioxin material is the fact that bio-assays made on chick embryos in another study revealed that all the embryos were killed by one twenty-millionth of a gram of dioxin per egg.

Perhaps an even more disquieting speculation about the dioxin is that 2,4,5-T may not be the only material in which it appears. Among the compounds that several experienced biologists and toxicologists suspect might contain or produce dioxin are the trichlorophenols and pentachlorophenols, which are rather widely present in the environment in various forms. For example, a number of the trichlorophenols and pentachlorophenols are used as slime-killing agents in paper-pulp manufacture, and are present in a wide range of consumer products, including adhesives, water-based and oil-based paints, varnishes and lacquers, and paper and paper coatings. They are used to prevent slime in pasteurizers and fungus on vats in breweries and are also used in hair shampoo. Along with the 2,4,5-T used in the Bionetics study, one trichlorophenol and one pentachlorophenol were tested without teratogenic results. But Dr. McLaughlin points out that since there are many such compounds put out by various companies, these particular samples might turn out to be—by the reasoning of the allegation that the 2,4,5-T used by Bionetics was unusually dirty—unusually clean.

Dr. McLaughlin tends to consider significant, in view of the now known extreme toxicity and possible extreme teratogenicity of dioxin, the existence of even very small amounts of the trichlorophenols and pentachlorophenols in food wrappings and other consumer products. Since the production of dioxin appears to be associated with high-temperature conditions, a question arises whether these thermal conditions are met at *any* stage of production or subsequent use or disposal of such materials, even in minute amounts. One of the problems here seems to be, as Dr. Epstein has put it, "The moment you introduce something into the environment it's likely to be burned sooner or later— that's the way we get rid of nearly everything." And most of these consumer products may wind up in municipal incinerators, and when they are burned, the thermal and other conditions for creating dioxin materials may quite possibly be met. If so, this could mean a release of dioxin material into the entire environment through the atmosphere.

Yet so far the dioxin material now suspected of causing the fetus-deforming effects in experimental animals has never been put through any formal teratological tests by any company or any government agency. If the speculation over the connection between dioxin in 2,4,5-T and the deaths of millions of baby chicks is borne out, it might mean that, quite contrary to the assumptions made up to now that 2,4,5-T is rapidly decomposable in soil, the dioxin material may be extremely persistent as well as extremely deadly.

So far, nobody knows—and it is probable that nobody will know for some time—whether the fetus deformities in the Bionetics study were caused by the 2,4,5-T itself, by the dioxin contaminant, or by some other substance or substances present in the 2,4,5-T, or whether human fetuses react to 2,4,5-T in the same way as the fetuses of the experimental animals in the Bionetics study. However, the experience so far with the employment of 2,4,5-T and substances chemically allied to it ought to be instructive. The history of 2,4,5-T is related to preparations for biological warfare, although nobody in the United States government seems to want to admit this, and it has wound up being used for purposes of biological warfare, although nobody in the United States government seems to want to admit *this,* either. Since 2,4,5-T was developed, the United States government has allowed it to be used on a very large scale on our own fields and countryside without adequate tests of its effects. In South Vietnam—a nation we are attempting to save—over a period of nine years the American military has sprayed or dumped this biological-warfare material on the countryside, on villages, and on South Vietnamese men and women in staggering amounts. In that time, the military has sprayed or dumped on Vietnam *50,000 tons* of herbicide, of which 20,000 tons have apparently been straight 2,4,5-T. In addition, the American military has apparently made incursions into a neutral country, Cambodia, and rained down on an area inhabited by 30,000 civilians a vast quantity of 2,4,5-T. Yet in the quarter of a century since the Department of Defense first developed the biological-warfare uses of this material it has not completed a single series of formal teratological tests on pregnant animals to determine whether it has an effect on their unborn offspring.

Similarly, officials of the Dow Chemical Company, one of the largest producers of 2,4,5-T, although they refuse to divulge how much 2,4,5-T they are and have been producing, admit that in all the years that they had produced the chemical before the DuBridge statement they had never made formal teratological tests on their 2,4,5-T, which they are now doing. The Monsanto Chemical Company, another big producer, had, as far as is known, never made such tests, either, nor, according to an official in the White House, had any other manufacturer. The Department of Agriculture has never required any such tests from manufacturers. The Food and Drug Administration has never required any such tests from manufacturers. The first tests to determine the teratogenic effects of 2,4,5-T were not made until the National Institutes of Health contracted for them with Bionetics Laboratories. And even then, when the adverse results of the tests became apparent, it was, as Dr. Epstein said, like "pulling teeth" to get the data out of the institutions involved. And when the data were obtained and the White House was obliged, partly by outside pressure and publicity, to act, the President's science adviser publicly presented the facts in a less than candid manner, while the Department of Defense, for all practical purposes, ignored the whole business and announced its intention of going on doing what it had been doing all along.

There have been a number of reports from Vietnam both of animal abortions and of malformed human babies that are thought to have resulted from spraying operations in which 2,4,5-T was used. But such scattered reports, however well founded, cannot really shed much more light on the situation. The fact is that even in this country, the best-fed, richest, and certainly most statistics-minded of all countries on earth, the standards for testing materials that are put into the environment, into drugs, and into the human diet are grossly inadequate. The screening system is so coarse that, as a teratology panel of the Mrak Commission warned recently, in connection with thalidomide, "the teratogenicity of thalidomide might have been missed had it not produced malformations rarely encountered." In other words, had it not been for the fact that very unusual and particularly terrible malformations appeared in an obvious pattern—for example, similarly malformed babies in the same hospital at about the same time—pregnant women might still be using thalidomide, and lesser deformations would, so to speak, disappear into the general statistical background. As for more subtle effects, such as brain damage and damage to the central nervous system, they would probably never show up as such at all. If such risks existed under orderly, normal medical conditions in a highly developed country, how is one ever to measure the harm that might be done to unborn children in rural Vietnam, in the midst of the malnutrition, the disease, the trauma, the poverty, and the general shambles of war?

2

The Official Position

New York
March 5, 1970

The Editors, *The New Yorker,*
Dear Sirs:

In an article that appeared in *The New Yorker* on February 7, I wrote that Dr. Lee DuBridge, the President's science adviser, issued a statement last October at the White House saying that because a laboratory study had shown a "higher than expected number of deformities" in the fetuses of mice and rats exposed to the herbicide 2,4,5-T, agencies of the United States government would take action to restrict the use of that substance in this country and in Vietnam, where it was being used in extensive military defoliation operations. This action, Dr. DuBridge announced, would include the cancellation, by January 1 of this year of Department of Agriculture permits for the use of 2,4,5-T on some American food crops unless the Food and Drug Administration had by then been able to determine a safe concentration of the herbicide in foods. Dr. DuBridge further announced that the Department of Defense would thenceforth "restrict the use of 2,4,5-T to areas remote from the population" in Vietnam. His statement added that these actions and others "will assure the safety of the public while further evidence [of the alleged harmful effects of 2,4,5-T] is being sought."

Four months have passed, and 2,4,5-T is still being used as widely as ever. The Department of Agriculture has yet to cancel its permits for the use of the herbicide on food crops in this country, and the Department of Defense is continuing to use it in populated areas of Vietnam. In the meantime, officials of the Dow Chemical Company, which is one of the largest producers of 2,4,5-T, have been maintaining that the samples of 2,4,5-T used in the study cited by Dr. DuBridge, which was done by the Bionetics Research Laboratories, of Bethesda, Maryland, were uncharacteristic of the 2,4,5-T currently being produced, because the material tested by Bionetics—which did not come from Dow—was contaminated to an unusual extent by a toxic substance identified as symmetrical 2,3,7,8-tetra-chlorodibenzo-p-dioxin. This contaminant, usually called dioxin, was alleged by the Dow people to be present in the Bionetics samples at a concentration of approximately twenty-seven parts per million, and they claim that the 2,4,5-T that Dow is currently producing contains the dioxin contaminant in concentrations of less than one part per million. The Dow people maintain that their currently produced 2,4,5-T does not appear to have the effect of deforming rat fetuses. In January, a Dow official told the Department of Health, Education, and Welfare, "We strongly urge that action concerning the status of 2,4,5-T be held in abeyance until [Dow's] testing program is completed [in] April." The United States government's failure so far to place the promised restrictions on the use of 2,4,5-T in this country may in part be attributed to this plea.

Because of the seriousness of the issues involved, it seems to me that the government's failure to act on the use of 2,4,5-T here and in Vietnam calls for much fuller public discussion. Even though the dioxin contaminant may now be present in 2,4,5-T in what the Dow Chemical Company apparently considers to be no more than tolerable amounts, the substance is of such potency that its release even in small concentrations must prompt deep concern. In the presumably more heavily dioxin-contaminated samples of 2,4,5-T that were used in the Bionetics work, the smallest dosages of 2,4,5-T that the test animals were given caused extensive deformities in fetuses. In more recent studies of the dioxin contaminant, conducted by Dr. Jacqueline Verrett, of the Food and Drug Administration (who earlier was responsible for revealing the carcinogenicity of cyclamates), extensive teratogenic, or fetus-deforming, effects were discovered in chick embryos when the dioxin, or a distillate predominantly consisting of it, was present at concentrations of little more than a trillionth of a gram per gram of the egg. The magnitude of this effect on chick embryos may be gathered from the fact that, according to Dr. Verrett's studies, the dioxin appears to be a million times as potent a fetus-deforming agent as the notorious teratogen thalidomide was found to be in tests on chicks. Of course, chick embryos are far down the biological ladder from human fetuses, and they are also extremely sensitive to many substances. But even if, for theoretical purposes, we reduced the teratogenic power of the dioxin, as shown in Dr. Verrett's chick-embryo studies, approximately a million times, we would *still* have to consider that we were dealing with a substance as teratogenically potent as thalidomide. That the United States government permits the presence, even in minute amounts, of such a substance in herbicidal mixtures to be sold for spraying on food crops and on suburban lawns—where some of the chemical may enter shallow wells and other drinking-water supplies—is hardly reassuring. And it is particularly disturbing when one reflects that in the quarter of a century in which 2,4,5-T was used prior to Dr. DuBridge's announcement not a single regulatory agency of the United States government, not the Department of Defense—which has been spreading huge quantities of 2,4,5-T on vast areas of Vietnam—and not, as far as is known, the researchers for any one of the half-dozen large American chemical companies producing the material had ever so much as opened up a pregnant mouse to determine whether 2,4,5-T or the dioxin contaminant in it did any systemic or pathogenic harm to the fetus. Several studies of the sort are now under way, but the United States government still seems to take the position that the 2,4,5-T produced by Dow and other large chemical companies should be considered innocent until it is proved to be otherwise. Meanwhile, 2,4,5-T is being sprayed on certain crops and on areas where it may come into contact with human beings, cattle, and wildlife. In Vietnam, it is still being sprayed by the military in concentrations that average thirteen times as great as those that the manufacturers themselves recommend as safe and effective for use in this country.

It is true that the teratogenicity of dioxin—as distinct from dioxin-contaminated 2,4,5-T—has not yet been established in tests conducted on experimental animals of mammalian species. However, the direct toxic, or body-poisoning, effects—as distinct from fetus-deforming effects—of dioxin are known to be very high both in animals and in human beings. In past studies on rats, dosages of forty-five millionths of a gram per kilo of the mother's body weight have been found to kill fifty per cent of the offspring. When dioxin was given orally to pregnant rats in recent tests, it was found, on preliminary investigation, to kill all fetuses with dosages of eight millionths of a gram per kilo of the mother's body weight, and to damage fetuses with dosages of a half-millionth of a gram per kilo.

Further, the effects of dioxin on human beings, even in small dosages, are known to be serious. In the past, in plants manufacturing 2,4,5-T an illness called chloracne seems to have been widespread among the workers. In the mid-sixties, Dow was obliged to close down part of a 2,4,5-T plant in Midland, Michigan, for some time because about sixty workers contracted chloracne as a result of contact with dioxin, which seems to be always present in varying degrees during the process of manufacturing 2,4,5-T and in the finished 2,4,5-T itself. The symptoms of this disease include extensive skin eruptions, disorders of the central nervous system, chronic fatigue, lassitude, and depression. Workers at a 2,4,5-T plant in New Jersey run by another company suffered similar symptoms in the mid-sixties, and six years later some of them were reported to be still suffering from the effects of the disease. In Germany, since the mid-fifties, workers in factory after factory producing 2,4,5-T and polychlorinated phenolic compounds have been afflicted with chloracne after absorbing apparently only minute amounts of the dioxin contaminant; their symptoms have been described in several medical papers as including liver damage, nervous and mental disorders, depression, loss of appetite and weight, and markedly reduced sexual drive.

When a reporter approached an official in Dr. DuBridge's office for information on 2,4,5-T, he was told that he would be given White House cooperation "only to a certain extent," because the official didn't want "wild speculation" stirred up. He cited as an example of "wild speculation" the recent controversy over the birth-control pill, which, he said, had "caused millions of women to get hysterical with worry." The reporter replied that he didn't think the analogy between 2,4,5-T and the Pill was a particularly good one, for the reason that a woman using the Pill could employ alternative methods of contraception, whereas a Vietnamese woman exposed to herbicidal spray put down by the American military had no choice in the matter.

But perhaps the comparison between 2,4,5-T (and its dioxin contaminant) and commonly used pills is worth pursuing. Suppose that such a dangerous substance as dioxin were found to be contained in a pill offered for human consumption in this country, and suppose that the contaminant were present in such minute amounts that an adult following the prescribed dosages might ingest a hundredth of a millionth of a gram of the contaminant per day. There is no doubt whatever that, according to existing Food and Drug Administration standards, the F.D.A. would immediately ban production and sale of the pill on the ground that it was highly dangerous to public health; in fact, the amount of such a potent contaminant that the F.D.A. would permit in a pill under the agency's present policy on toxicity would almost certainly be zero.

While 2,4,5-T, with or without the dioxin contaminant, doesn't come in pill form, it may be worthwhile to try to calculate, on the basis of a hypothetical pill, how much 2,4,5-T (and dioxin) a Vietnamese woman living in an area sprayed by the American military might ingest in a day. It has already been calculated by reputable biologists that, if one takes into account the average amount of 2,4,5-T sprayed per acre in Vietnam, and also takes into account a one-inch rainfall—such as is common there—after a spraying, a forty-kilo (about eighty-eight-pound) Vietnamese woman drinking two liters (about two quarts) of 2,4,5-T-contaminated water per day could be ingesting about 120 milligrams (about a two-hundred-and-fiftieth of an ounce) of 2,4,5-T a day. If the 2,4,5-T contained the dioxin contaminant at a level of one part per million—which is what the Dow people say is the maximum amount present in the 2,4,5-T they are currently producing—the Vietnamese woman would be absorbing a little over a tenth of a microgram of dioxin per day, or ten times the amount of dioxin entering the system of an adult from the hypothetical pill that the F.D.A. would certainly find dangerous to human health. Further, if this Vietnamese woman were to conceive a child two weeks, say, after the spraying, the weight of the dioxin that by these same calculations would have then accumulated in her system (the evidence thus far is that dioxin accumulates in mammalian tissue in the same manner as the chlorinated hydrocarbons, such as DDT) would be more than the weight of the just-fertilized ovum. Considering the existing evidence of the frightening degree of teratogenicity of the dioxin in chick embryos and its highly toxic effects on mammalian fetuses, the presence of this much dioxin in a mother's body at the very beginning of a human life surely has ominous implications.

Now, what about the safety of 2,4,5-T itself? Admittedly, the dioxin contaminant seems to be a residue from one stage of its manufacture. But if by some future chemical miracle the very last trace of dioxin could be removed from the finished 2,4,5-T, would the resultant "pure" 2,4,5-T be harmless? The fact seems to be that even then 2,4,5-T, as produced in this country, would have to be viewed with suspicion, for the breakdown products of 2,4,5-T, when subjected to heat and other conditions, are themselves capable, according to a number of responsible biologists, of producing dioxin. Given this potential, the ultimate folly in our defoliation operations in Vietnam was possibly achieved during 1965 and 1966, when the military made large-scale efforts in two defoliated areas to create fire storms—that is, fires so huge that all the oxygen in those areas would be exhausted. The apparent intention was to render the soil barren. (A fire storm would also, of course, have the result of burning or suffocating any living beings remaining in the area.) Operation Sherwood Forest, conducted in 1965, was an attempt to burn a defoliated section of the Boi Loi Woods. In October, 1966, the military began Operation Pink Rose, a similar project. Neither of the projects, in which tons of napalm were thrown down on top of the residue of tons of sprayed 2,4,5-T, succeeded in creating the desired effect; whether they released into the atmosphere dioxin produced by the breakdown products of the 2,4,5-T will probably never be known.

There are also less spectacular ways in which conditions suitable for the release of dioxin in Vietnam may have been created. For example, after areas accessible by road have been defoliated, woodcutters move in to chop up the dead timber, which is then sold in nearby towns and villages as fuel in the form of charcoal or firewood. Large quantities of fuel derived from defoliated areas are said to have been entering Saigon for years. Since the fires are customarily tended by Vietnamese women, and since many of them are certainly pregnant, the hazards to health and to the lives of unborn children surely cannot be ignored.

In the United States, the potential hazards from the present use of 2,4,5-T are considerably less than they are in Vietnam. In the first place, the recommended concentrations of 2,4,5-T for spraying here are, as I have pointed out, about a thirteenth of what the Vietnamese population is sometimes subjected to. And, in the second place, a great deal, if not most, of the 2,4,5-T that would otherwise have been sprayed on American crops and grazing areas has for several years been sent to Vietnam. However, the shortage of 2,4,5-T in this country does not necessarily mean that the potential hazards are at a minimum. The substances known as the trichlorophenols and compounds of pentachlorophenol, which officials of the F.D.A. believe may be chemical precursors of dioxin under certain thermal and other conditions, are used widely in the manufacture of a large variety of consumer products, ranging from paper to laundry starch and hair shampoo. Dow Chemical puts out a whole line of polychlorophenolic chemicals known as Dowicide Products. Monsanto Chemical also puts out a line of pentachlorophenol substances, known as Penta Compounds. Since a very great many consumer products wind up being burned sooner or later, and since the polychlorophenolic compounds are suspected of being capable, under particular thermal and other conditions, of releasing dioxin, the alarming question arises whether, and to what extent, dioxin is being released into the environment through the atmosphere. Pentachlorophenol, used in certain herbicides, is readily decomposed in sunlight, and in its breakdown process a number of products, including chemical precursors of chlorodibenzo-p-dioxin compounds, are produced. Because of these factors, a whole range of pesticides, as well as of herbicides, now must come under suspicion of producing dioxin compounds.

Although the chemical companies that manufacture 2,4,5-T have long taken pride in pointing out that 2,4,5-T itself is quite readily decomposable in soil, the crucial matters of how stable the dioxin contaminant is and to what extent it is cumulative in animal tissue have apparently been neglected. Consequently, the fact that traces of compounds virtually indistinguishable from dioxin have already been detected in this country in the human food chain—in the livers of chickens and in edible oils —clearly indicates that dioxin should be considered a hazard to man. Why, under all these inauspicious circumstances, the production and the use here and in Vietnam of 2,4,5-T has not summarily been stopped by the United States government is hard to understand.

3

Hazards at Home

New York
June 7, 1970

The Editors, *The New Yorker,*
Dear Sirs:

In the issues of February 7 and March 14 of this year, I presented in *The New Yorker* some of the mounting evidence regarding the dangerous teratogenic, or fetus-deforming, effects of the herbicide 2,4,5-T, which has been used in huge amounts over the past decade as a defoliant in Vietnam and as a weed killer here at home. What seemed particularly alarming, as I reported, was the seemingly unavoidable presence in 2,4,5-T of a highly toxic and teratogenic contaminant belonging to a group known commonly as dioxins. I also pointed out the reluctance of the government, despite its apparent awareness of the dangers, to eliminate or drastically restrict the use of this herbicide.

On April 15, the Surgeon General of the United States, Dr. Jesse L. Steinfeld, appeared before a Senate subcommittee, headed by Senator Philip A. Hart, of Michigan, that was investigating the safety of 2,4,5-T and announced, on behalf of the Secretary of the Interior, the Secretary of Agriculture, and the Secretary of Health, Education, and Welfare, a number of measures that were being taken to limit the use of 2,4,5-T in this country. These measures included the immediate suspension of the Department of Agriculture's registrations of liquid formulations of 2,4,5-T used around the home and of all formulations used for killing vegetation around lakes, ponds, and irrigation ditches. The Surgeon General also announced that the Department of Agriculture was about to cancel its registrations of nonliquid formulations of 2,4,5-T for use around the home and on food crops, including corn, barley, oats, rice, rye, apples, and blueberries. On the same day, Deputy Secretary of Defense David Packard announced the immediate suspension of the use of 2,4,5-T in Vietnam.

Against a background of evidence accumulated since 1966 that 2,4,5-T, or material with which it is ordinarily contaminated to some degree, exerts a fetus-deforming effect on the offspring of experimental animals, and a background, too, of extraordinary reluctance on the part of government agencies, including the office of President Nixon's own science adviser, Dr. Lee DuBridge, to inform the public in a forthright manner about the potential hazards of 2,4,5-T to human health, the statement by the Surgeon General appeared to signal clear and unequivocal action at last against the widespread use of 2,4,5-T. Federal law requires that all pesticides and herbicides be registered with the Department of Agriculture before they can be marketed in interstate commerce, and the conclusion that citizens could reasonably be expected to draw from the Surgeon General's statement was that cancellation and suspension of these registrations had put an immediate stop to the sale and use of 2,4,5-T here.

That conclusion, I regret to say, is not justified. The word "cancellation," which has such an air of finality about it, and which seems to signify drastic action, is really one of the weaker words in the federal-regulatory lexicon—far weaker than the word "suspension," which the Department of Agriculture has applied to its action on the registrations of liquid formulations of 2,4,5-T used around the home and around lakes, ponds, and irrigation ditches. To illustrate one of the powerful distinctions implicit in this upside-down bureaucratic language, when the

Department of Agriculture *suspends* the registration of a product for certain uses, the suspension takes force immediately, and under federal law shipments of the product in interstate commerce must stop; in effect, the flow of the product from manufacturer to ultimate user is immediately pinched off at a point reasonably close to the source of supply. When the Department of Agriculture *cancels* the registration of a product for certain uses, however, the movement of the product in interstate commerce is brought to no such automatic halt. A company given a cancellation order is told that after thirty days it can no longer ship its product across state lines, but the company has the right to appeal the order, and if it does appeal, this action has the effect of staying the order. During the lengthy process of appeal, the company can continue to produce, ship, and sell the canceled product. A company whose product's registration is suspended has no such recourse.

Approximately six weeks after the Surgeon General's announcement concerning 2,4,5-T, I stopped in at several garden stores in the New York area. I found that a number of 2,4,5-T formulations—weed killers, poison-ivy sprays, and lawn food—were still on sale. Since the Surgeon General had cited as one of the primary reasons for federal actions against 2,4,5-T the government's wish to afford "maximum protection to women in the childbearing years" by preventing them from being exposed to the herbicide, this state of affairs startled me, particularly since May and June are the months of maximum use of herbicides. The disturbing fact is that the Department of Agriculture has no power to compel manufacturers to recall from retail stores products whose registration for certain uses the Department has either canceled *or* suspended. There is no federal law against a retailer's selling such a product or against a customer's buying it. The law does provide that stocks of it can be seized by Department of Agriculture inspectors. However, the number of retail establishments selling herbicidal formulations for home use runs into the scores of thousands, whereas the number of retail-store inspectors employed by the Department of Agriculture, I recently discovered, is exactly thirty-two. On a practical level, then, the power of the Department of Agriculture to prevent the retail sale of such products is almost nonexistent. Furthermore, not only is it legal under federal law for a homeowner to buy a product whose registration for certain uses has been officially canceled or suspended but it is legal for him to use it, and use it in any way he pleases. Without breaking any federal law, he can dump concentrations of 2,4,5-T on his lawn in such a way that some of it enters his or his neighbors' water supplies.

Similarly, a farmer can continue to use 2,4,5-T on his crops without breaking any federal law even though that use has been the subject of a Department of Agriculture cancellation order. The only risk he faces is that of seizure by Food and Drug Administration inspectors of any of his crops shipped in interstate commerce that are found to have detectable amounts of 2,4,5-T residue on them. The risk isn't a very great one, since these inspections take place at retail outlets—supermarkets, and so on—where F.D.A. inspectors collect samples of foodstuff and send them back to the F.D.A. for analysis, which takes time. The bureaucratic machinery is creaky, and if any detectable residue of 2,4,5-T is found on the foodstuff—say, blueberries that the farmer has sprayed with 2,4,5-T—the chances are that by the time the government is ready to seize the stock of blueberries in the store (which, after all, is probably only one of many stores to which berries from this batch have been shipped) the blueberries have been bought and eaten. In any event, only the blueberries can be found guilty—not the farmer or the shipper. And the farmer can go right on using 2,4,5-T as he pleases, because the cancellation powers and suspension powers of the Department of Agriculture apply not to the basic chemical compound of 2,4,5-T as such but only to the formally registered *uses* for which it is intended. In effect, this means that there is federal control only over the wording of labels on the cans, bottles, or drums of these chemicals. It is true that the Department has asked manufacturers of 2,4,5-T products whose registration for certain uses has been canceled or suspended to recall the products from retailers, but this will have to be done strictly on a voluntary basis if it is done at all. Even if it actually is done, and the products are back in the manufacturers' hands, the recall does not mean that the 2,4,5-T will be destroyed. For the most part, it means merely that the 2,4,5-T formulation will be relabeled, with the canceled uses deleted, and sold over again in the same form, and even in the same containers. And since the label on the container has no binding force on the purchaser, there is no guarantee at all that 2,4,5-T will not continue to be applied in ways that the public might reasonably suppose to have been stopped dead by the government.

Further examination reveals that the measures against the use of 2,4,5-T that appear to be so sweeping actually apply to about ten per cent of the total amount of 2,4,5-T used in this country—that is, only to 2,4,5-T used around homes, gardens, and aquatic areas and on food crops. And since 2,4,5-T products are still being sold freely in garden-supply stores, I estimate that so far the cancellation and suspension orders have affected no more than two or three per cent of the total amount. About ninety per cent, in any case, is used for the control of woody plants in such areas as rangeland and pastureland and along railroad and electric-line rights-of-way. These uses remain unaffected by the new federal orders because the Departments of Agriculture, H.E.W., and the Interior agreed that in such areas, many of which are remote from dense population, 2,4,5-T does not constitute an imminent hazard to women of childbearing age.

I believe that this conclusion deserves reexamination. As studies with experimental animals have shown, 2,4,5-T is a fetus-deforming agent both in its relatively pure form, which has so far been formulated only under laboratory-test conditions, and in the form in which it is ordinarily sold to users. Because certain factors are apparently impossible to eliminate in its production, the latter form is a contaminated one, the contaminants being present in amounts that have up to now been considered tolerable. The name of the principal contaminant in 2,4,5-T is symmetrical 2,3,7,8-tetrachlorodibenzo-*p*-dioxin, and it has been found to be both extremely toxic and, in certain tests on living creatures, teratogenic. In tests on chick embryos, this form of dioxin, in a pure state, has the capacity to deform embryos at levels of a trillionth of a gram per kilogram of the egg—a level only one-millionth as great as that required to achieve a comparable effect in chick-embryo experiments with the notorious teratogen thalidomide. And in tests involving a mixture of dioxins in which the symmetrical 2,3,7,8-tetrachlo-rodibenzo-*p*-dioxin predominated, conducted by the Food and Drug Administration on pregnant hamsters, a dosage of 9.1 millionths of a gram per day (for five days) per kilogram of the mother's body weight produced an incidence of eighty-two per cent mortality and eighty-two per cent abnormality among live offspring.

Dioxin contaminants are also known to have untoward effects on human beings. In factories where 2,4,5-T is produced, the dioxin appears as a contaminant in an intermediate stage of the manufacturing process, and some of its remains in the finished product. In 1964, workers in a Midland, Michigan, factory of the Dow Chemical Company, one of the largest producers of 2,4,5-T, contracted an illness through exposure to the dioxin contaminant. The symptoms of this illness were described as follows by Dr. Julius E. Johnson, a vice-president of Dow Chemical and its director of research and development, in testimony he gave in mid-April before the Senate subcommittee investigating 2,4,5,-T:

> The most sensitive toxic reaction observed in humans to this impurity [the tetra dioxin] was manifested by a condition known as chloracne, a skin disorder mostly prevalent on the face, neck and back. It is similar in appearance to severe acne often suffered by teenagers.

The way Dr. Johnson described chloracne before the Senate subcommittee, it does not sound like a very serious condition. However, the way he described it before the subcommittee is not quite the way Dr. Benjamin Holder, the director of the medical department at Dow's Midland Division, had described it two months earlier during a meeting with government chemists. According to a memorandum originating in one of the regulatory agencies involved, Dr. Holder said that about sixty people had contracted the disease at the Dow plant, and that its onset had been slow—four to six weeks. The memorandum continued:

Early symptoms [according to Dr. Holder] include fatigue, lassitude and depression, and early signs include the appearance of comedones on the face and body . . . and weight loss. . . . Severe exposure results in effects involving internal organs and nervous system disorder (polyneuritis). . . . Dr. Holder discussed the examination and treatment of exposed workers. He said that six months were required for marked recovery to begin, and complete recovery required up to several years.

According to a paper published in a German scientific journal a year before the Dow people made these observations, the symptoms of chloracne associated with the intermediate stage of manufacture of 2,4,5-T include mental depression, reduced power of recall and concentration, disturbed sleep, irritability, reduced libido, and impotence. And another scientific paper, so far unpublished, on an outbreak of chloracne that occurred in another 2,4,5-T factory (not a Dow factory) in the United States, describes the continued existence of serious mental disturbance among affected workers some six years afterward. The reason I emphasize the presence and the extremely hazardous nature of the dioxin contaminant in 2,4,5-T is that while the Dow people claim that 2,4,5-T is readily decomposable in soil and by the action of sunlight after it has been applied, neither they nor anyone else has ever shown that the dioxin contaminant, as distinct from a theoretically pure 2,4,5-T, is biologically degradable; that is, that it does not persist in the environment or accumulate in animal tissue. On the contrary, the characteristics of dioxin-related chloracne poisoning, far from resembling those of the transient acne of teen-agers, include effects that are surely indicative of a serious toxic influence that is stubbornly persistent in the human body and its central nervous system. And, according to Dr. Jacqueline Verrett, of the Food and Drug Administration (Dr. Verrett's chick-embryo studies contributed to the discovery that the cyclamates widely used as sugar sub-

stitutes were carcinogenic substances), studies of the effects
of dioxin compounds on chicks and small mammals indicate that
the tetra dioxin may very well accumulate in animal tissue more
or less as DDT does—the difference being that this dioxin is
infinitely more toxic.

In the absence of positive proof that dioxin is not persistent
and cumulative, the continued virtually unrestricted spraying of
2,4,5-T on pastureland and rangeland seems to me to constitute
a serious potential hazard to human health. In spite of manufacturers' claims, there appears to be no evidence that the
dioxin contaminant does not persist in the sprayed area long
after the 2,4,5-T itself has broken down. The amount of dioxin
that would thus remain would, admittedly, be very small in
relation to the amount of 2,4,5-T originally laid down—the Dow
people, for example, claim that the dioxin content of their
2,4,5-T is less than one part per million—but the potency of
dioxin is so extreme that a serious question arises whether traces
of dioxin may not remain on sprayed pastureland and be ingested
by beef cattle, dairy cows, and sheep, with the result that dioxin
may build up in the tissues of the livestock and enter the human
food chain through meat or milk. The relentlessness of the
cumulative process involving DDT and other pesticides is well
known by now, when human milk contains more DDT than
federal law permits in cow's milk crossing state lines, and when
virtually every sample of drinking water tested throughout the
country by the Environmental Control Administration has contained traces of pesticide. The only precaution recommended by
the Department of Agriculture against possible contamination of
dairy cattle feeding on pastureland sprayed with 2,4,5-T is that
the land not be grazed for seven days after a spraying. Since
the Department's own calculations of the persistence of 2,4,5-T
—calculations that take no account whatever of the persistence
of the dioxin contaminant—are that 2,4,5-T takes about five
months to break down in soil, these precautionary measures as
they relate to grass growing from the soil or water holes on its
surface hardly seem adequate for the ultimate protection of the
public against a herbicide that has been demonstrated to be a

serious potential health hazard even in a laboratory-purified form. As for precautions against the ingestion of dioxin, there simply aren't any, because as far as federal regulations are concerned dioxin does not exist. In the case of grazing beef cattle, the Department of Agriculture does not recommend withholding the land from use for as much as a day after a 2,4,5-T spraying. In Texas alone, more than a million acres of rangeland and pastureland are being sprayed with 2,4,5-T this year; probably at least a quarter of a million head of cattle will graze on that sprayed land; and the cattle will produce something like a hundred and fifty million pounds of meat that will be sold to Americans as edible—all in the absence of a solitary meaningful restriction imposed by the federal government on either the spraying or the grazing, and also in the absence of a solitary scientific study, either by industry or by any government agency, concerning the stability, the persistence, and the cumulative capacity of the dioxin contaminant in the bodies of living creatures.

Next year, the total area sprayed with 2,4,5-T throughout the country may well be greatly increased rather than decreased. The use of herbicides in this country has been increasing at a considerably greater rate than that of pesticides, and it is only because military priorities for defoliation programs in Vietnam cut the available suply of 2,4,5-T quite drastically that this country has been spared the much more extensive use of 2,4,5-T on rangeland and pastureland. In Vietnam, a total of about forty million pounds of 2,4,5-T has been dropped on the countryside. The suspension, under public pressure, of the use of 2,4,5-T there will probably bring about the release in the coming year of huge amounts of it in the domestic market, and a logical target of chemical-company salesmen for disposal of the surplus would be the cattle industry and the United States Forest Service.

Also, to my knowledge, no proper investigation has ever been made of the possibility that, quite aside from the dioxin already present in 2,4,5-T sprayed on vegetation, *further* amounts of dioxin may be created, and released into the environment, through the breakdown process of 2,4,5-T as it is affected by sunlight and by heat. Heat strong enough to create new dioxin can occur under conditions that are not highly unusual. Brush that has been killed, whether by 2,4,5-T or other means, is certainly a fire hazard, especially in a hot, dry climate, such as that of Texas, where so much 2,4,5-T spraying is going on, and a brush fire over a large sprayed area containing 2,4,5-T residues could conceivably generate considerable quantities of dioxin and release it into the atmosphere.

It seems most likely that the hazards of pollution of the environment by dioxins extend far beyond the use of 2,4,5-T. This herbicide is only one of many products derived from polychlorinated phenolic compounds that contain dioxins or are the precursors of dioxins. These products range from pesticides to deodorants. It appears that when any chlorophenol is heated sufficiently it can be converted into a dioxin. This fact raises questions about the release of dioxins into the environment merely through the burning of many commonly used products. For example, one of the polychlorinated phenolic compounds, pentachlorophenol, is widely used as a fungicide and as an antibacterial preparation. It is used in preserving wood and in controlling slime in the manufacture of paper. In 1968, more than twenty-seven million pounds of pentachlorophenol and its salts were used in the United States to preserve wood. Since the fate of most timber is to be burned sooner or later, and since it is reported that when five grams of pentachlorophenol is heated at a temperature of three hundred degrees for twelve hours it is capable of generating one and a half grams of octachlorodibenzo-p-dioxin, the possibility that considerable amounts of dioxin will be released into the atmosphere from wood treated with this preservative presents a potential health hazard of very alarming dimensions. The same thing may be said of the burning of paper that has been treated with pentachlorophenol. Aside from any hazard created by burning, the extreme toxicity of pentachlorophenol was discussed some years ago in an article in the *British Medical Journal* on some sawmill workers in Borneo who handled wet timbers that had been freshly treated with a solution of sodium pentachlorophenate, a salt of pentachlorophenol. The people involved, who are described in a Monsanto Chemical Company manual on pentachlorophenol as "nine undernourished, scantily clothed native workers," were not wearing protective garments—a circumstance that the Monsanto manual calls a "complete violation of safety precautions for handling Penta [a Monsanto trade name] materials." They died as a result of handling the timbers.

Pentachlorophenol is used in a wide variety of products, including paints and shampoos. It is put in laundry starches as a preservative, and it has been used in other laundry products. The extreme hazards posed by the injudicious use of this chemical, which is buried in so many consumer products, can be perceived in a scientific paper that appeared in the *Journal of Pediatrics* last August, entitled "Pentachlorophenol Poisoning in a Nursery for Newborn Infants." The paper describes the cases of nine infants between six and fourteen days old who were all born in a small hospital for unmarried mothers in St. Louis and who were all admitted to St. Louis Children's Hospital with a severe form of an unusual and undiagnosed illness marked by excessive sweating, increased heart rate, respiratory difficulty, and enlargement of the liver. Two of the infants died shortly after being admitted to Children's Hospital; the rest were given blood transfusions and other treatment and survived. The cause of the poisoning was traced to an antimicrobial laundry neutralizer that had been used in excessive amounts in the laundry of the hospital where the children were born. The neutralizer contained sodium pentachlorophenate, and traces of pentachlorophenol that remained in diapers and other clothing after laundering had penetrated the skin of the infants and entered their systems. The insidious nature of pentachlorophenol can be illustrated further by the fact that after the use of the rinse was discontinued, traces of pentachlorophenol continued to be found in the blood of newborn children and of expectant mothers. It turned out that although the infants were no longer directly exposed to pentachlorophenol, the mothers-to-be had continued to use linens that had been rinsed with it.

There is speculation that the pentachlorophenol traces in the linens used by the expectant mothers became absorbed into their systems and crossed the placental barrier into the systems of the unborn babies.

Such facts led me to become curious about other commonly used products that contain polychlorinated phenolic compounds. One of these is the household disinfectant Lysol, which contains a chlorophenol compound. Another polychlorinated phenolic compound that is widely used is hexachlorophene. The basic material for hexachlorophene originates in 2,4,5-trichlorophenol, which is also the precursor of 2,4,5-T in the manufacture of the herbicide. Hexachlorophene is very widely used as an antibacterial agent, and is an ingredient of toilet soaps, of skin lotions for babies, and of cleaning powders used for washing diapers and infants' laundry. It is used in deodorant creams and sprays, and it is a principal active ingredient of pHisoHex, a sudsing antibacterial agent for the skin that is universally used in hospitals and widely used in homes. (In hospitals, it is used in scrubbing up before surgery.)

A relatively small number of people appear to be sensitive to such hexachlorophene preparations when they are applied to the skin, but the undoubted benefits of the preparations are generally considered to far outweigh this known disadvantage. Manufacturers of soap claim that hexachlorophene does not readily penetrate the natural barrier of the human skin. However, it may be another matter when hexachlorophene preparations are used where the natural skin barrier has been broken down. In 1965, at the Shriners' Burns Institute, a hospital in Galveston, affiliated with the University of Texas, that is devoted to the treatment of severe burns, nine children had their wounds cleansed with a three-per-cent solution of hexachlorophene in a detergent in preparation for skin grafts. Six of the children soon developed generalized convulsions. To determine the cause of the convulsions, a study was subsequently made in which hexachlorophene was sprinkled into skin incisions in rats. All the rats died.

More recently, Dr. Verrett has made studies of the effects of hexachlorophene on chick embryos, and her observations concerning one of her experiments have led her to conclude that hexachlorophene is so toxic that when it is injected into the embryos in a concentration of half a milligram per kilogram of egg it kills sixty per cent of the embryos. In another study, in which hexachlorophene was injected into the eggs at this same concentration, Dr. Verrett found signs of teratogenicity—including a significant incidence of cleft palate, eye and beak defects, and leg deformations and edemas, or body-fluid swellings —similar to the teratogenic effects she had found in comparable chick-embryo studies of 2,4,5,-T, of the dioxin contaminant, and of 2,4,5-trichlorophenol.

Hexachlorophene has been manufactured for commercial purposes for about thirty years, and last year between two and three million pounds was produced in this country; much larger quantities are expected to be available in 1970, again because of the suspension of the use of 2,4,5-T in Vietnam. The Food and Drug Administration places no restrictions on the use of hexachlorophene in such consumer products as toilet soap and deodorants. Yet, as far as I can determine, not one single series of formal tests has ever been completed either by any corporation or by any government agency to determine whether this chemical is teratogenic, whether it causes mutations, or whether it produces cancer in experimental animals. Regardless of this lack of data, the Department of Agriculture permits the use of hexachlorophene in certain pesticides used on farm produce. It is sprayed on certain fruits and vegetables to cut down bacterial action that might encourage spoilage. Its use is permitted in quite high concentrations in water drunk by livestock, as a means of preventing liver flukes in cattle. If it is effective against liver flukes in cattle, it presumably penetrates to the liver, and since beef and calf's liver winds up on the dinner table, one wonders about other ways in which hexachlorophene might possibly be ingested by humans. One route might be through drinking water. With the huge amounts of hexachlorophene used in soaps and such consumer products, regardless of whether, as soap manufacturers claim, very little of the hexachlorophene is absorbed into the human body through the skin, the hexachlorophene that remains outside the skin is for the most part drained away in waste water. Since much waste water in this country is reused, after treatment, as drinking water, it seems reasonable to question whether traces of hexachlorophene are ingested by human beings in this way.

Both the ubiquity of polychlorinated phenolic compounds in the environment and their apparent ability to accumulate in the systems of living creatures are suggested by the contamination caused by a group of polychlorinated phenolic compounds known as polychlorinated biphenyls, or, more commonly, PCBs. These materials, which are known to be highly toxic, and are potential sources of dioxins in themselves, are used for a wide variety of purposes. They are used in rubber products and insulating materials, in paper coatings, in brake linings, in asphalt tiles and other asphalt compounds, in paints and varnishes, in inks for high-speed presses, in waxes, and also in pesticides. In this country, PCBs are manufactured by the Monsanto Chemical Company under the trade name Aroclors. According to a recent article by Dr. Robert Risebrough, of the Institute of Marine Resources of the University of California at Berkeley, in the magazine *Environment,* PCBs have been found in North American peregrine falcons in amounts as great as 1,980 parts per million parts of body fat, and, in Sweden, in the fat of the white-tailed eagle in the amount of 17,000 parts per million. Traces of PCBs have been discovered in fish in Lake Michigan, and it may therefore be assumed that PCBs have found their way into the human food chain. In tests of samples of mothers' milk from Los Angeles and Berkeley that were analyzed late in 1968 by Dr. James Enderson, of Colorado College, every sample tested contained traces of PCBs.

Of the polychlorinated phenolic herbicides used in the United States, the most widely used is 2,4-dichlorophenoxyacetic acid, or 2,4-D. In 1968, approximately fifty-seven million pounds of 2,4-D was used in this country, in compounds that ranged from agricultural sprays to lawn foods and preparations for removing dandelions. As far as the Department of Agriculture is concerned, 2,4-D may be sprayed on virtually any crop or area—with minor restrictions as to intervals before harvesting, and so on. Last year, probably fifty-seven million acres of agricultural land was sprayed with it, and probably more than a million pounds of it was used on turf alone. Over the past ten years, close to half a billion pounds of 2,4-D has been laid down on vegetation in this country, and today every garden store is full of compounds containing it; about 175 companies produce 2,4-D preparations, and the chemical appears in somewhere between 500 and 800 products currently in use. In spite of the Department of Agriculture's almost completely permissive attitude toward the use of 2,4-D, this herbicide has never been proved to be non-hazardous to public health. Last year, 2,4-D was characterized in a report by the Bionetics Research Laboratories, in Bethesda, Maryland—the original discoverer of the teratogenic qualities of 2,4,5-T—as "potentially dangerous" and "needing further study." Recently, a screening study conducted by Dr. Verrett on the effects of purified 2,4-D on chick embryos showed the 2,4-D to have teratogenic effects. And preliminary observations in a study, also made within the F.D.A., of the effects of commercially produced 2,4-D given orally at high dosage levels to pregnant hamsters are said to show an incidence of birth abnormalities, including skeletal abnormalities, higher than that in studies of the effects of purified 2,4,5-T given to pregnant hamsters at comparable dosage levels. But the Department of Agriculture has made no move either to warn the public of these ominous findings or to restrict 2,4-D's registered uses.

The potential hazards of 2,4,5-T and 2,4-D were further underlined this spring by a report concerning the fate of a herd of six hundred reindeer on government rangeland near Luleå, in northern Sweden, which had been sprayed last July with a mixture of one part 2,4,5-T and two parts 2,4-D at the rate of a little less than two pounds per acre. A few weeks after the animals had eaten large amounts of sprayed foliage, a hundred of them died and another hundred and fifty disappeared—the presumption being that many of the missing ones also succumbed. Among the surviving animals, forty females had miscarriages. Analysis of the reindeer carcasses by the National Swedish Veterinary Institute showed significant residues of 2,4-D and 2,4,5-T in their kidneys and livers. In view of this report, the almost complete lack of restrictions by our Department of Agriculture on the use of 2,4,5-T and 2,4-D on rangeland and pastureland seems particularly disturbing.

The acute effects on human beings of high dosages of PCBs are evident from a series of outbreaks of poisoning, traced to cooking oil extracted from rice hulls, that occurred two years ago in western Japan, in which at least ten thousand people were affected. The outbreaks involved both an abnormal incidence of miscarriages and stillbirths among women in the affected population and abnormally dark skin pigmentation in infants. The victims of the poisoning showed the classic symptoms of chloracne, and in several very serious cases they also showed symptoms of jaundice and other liver damage. Polychlorinated phenolic compounds are known to be used in Japan as herbicides on paddy fields, and the causative agent of the poisoning was identified as a PCB. Yet our Department of Agriculture permits the use of PCBs as additives in between thirty and forty registered pesticide products and has taken no action to protect the public against the dangers of these additives.

It seems to me clear from all this that the whole family of polychlorinated phenolic compounds is one that, scientifically speaking, consistently produces very bad news. In spite of this, the federal agencies charged with regulating the use of such substances to protect public health have taken virtually no effective steps either to investigate the harmful potential of these compounds or to protect the public from such possible harm. The Department of Agriculture, which has jurisdiction over the pesticidal and other non-drug uses of all sterilizing, disinfecting, germicidal, and antibacterial chemicals sold in this country— and most of the polychlorinated phenols are in one or more of these categories—has not, during all the years in which it has permitted the use of these substances, completed one laboratory study of dioxin contamination or of dioxin generation by any polychlorinated phenol. After almost a quarter of a century during which the Department has authorized the virtually unrestricted use of a herbicidal agent as powerful as 2,4,5-T, and in the face of well-established facts about the alarming teratogenicity both of 2,4,5-T and of its dioxin contaminant, none of the scientists employed by the Department have completed a single working experiment on the prevalence and generation of dioxins. Although they have gone so far as to draw up a list of seventeen polychlorinated phenolic compounds that they believe should be studied, they do not know, at the time this is written, even how many formulations of these compounds are on the market, what quantities of them are being sold, and what uses they are being put to. I became aware of this when, before writing this letter, I called the Pesticides Regulation Division of the Department of Agriculture and asked for a list of registered products containing polychlorinated phenolic compounds. According to the assistant director of the Pesticides Regulation Division, the Department has no such list and no list of formulators in whose names the products have been registered, nor has it a list of the uses to which the compounds in interstate commerce are being put. No one had ever before asked for such a list, he said, and the only way the Department could compile one for me would be by making a manual search through files containing some fifty thousand pesticidal-product registrations—which would, of course, be very expensive and complicated.

Clearly, in the polychlorinated phenolic compounds, we are confronted with substances in our environment that, even though we may be exposed to any of them in almost undetectable quantities, cumulatively and collectively pose frightening potential hazards to public health and involve the serious question of possible effects on the unborn. Considering the striking contrast between the urgency of the problems and the apparent inability of federal regulatory agencies to take prompt action to protect the public against these hazards, it seems to me that a drastic change in methods is essential. The existing pattern of inertia is attributable to a complex set of circumstances that includes inadequate statutory authority to deal with potentially hazardous products on the necessary environmental scale—all the way from their creation in factories, through their movement in interstate commerce, to their use and their eventual disposal or decomposition. A second factor is the very inadequate funding by Congress of the regulatory agencies. The Food and Drug Administration, for example, is supposed properly to regulate various activities of businesses that gross some three hundred *billion* dollars a year on an annual departmental budget of sixty million dollars, while the Department of Agriculture, as I have pointed out, has those thirty-two retail-store inspectors to cover the whole country. These conditions account, in part, for the passive attitude that agencies often take toward the industries they are supposed to regulate. Once a product has been registered as acceptable for use in interstate commerce, it tends to acquire such status that if subsequent questions arise about its safety, the burden of proof concerning this is really placed upon the federal regulatory agency rather than on the producer of the product. Since the agency too often does not have adequate facilities, money, or manpower to offer such proof, general foot-dragging or tired surrender to industry pressure by the agency people is naturally encouraged. It seems to me grossly improper that doubts raised about the safety of complex chemical substances put out by large companies for extensive public use should be so often resolved by federal regulatory agencies in favor of the welfare of these companies rather than of the welfare of the public. It does appear to me that in the case of the present uses of 2,4,5-T, 2,4-D, and other polychlorinated phenolic herbicide or pesticide compounds, such doubts can best be resolved by simply imposing a full suspension of all uses of these chemicals until it has been shown, as clearly as science can demonstrate through the necessary chemical, biological, and environmental testing, that the employment of these substances or their contaminants or breakdown products will not be hazardous to public health.

4

Special Military
and Industrial Interests

New York
June 24, 1970

The Editors, *The New Yorker,*
Dear Sirs:

In the pages of *The New Yorker* in February, in March, and earlier this month, I discussed evidence of the potential hazards to human beings, including those still to be born, from the use of the herbicides 2,4,5-T and 2,4-D. Thanks to the pressure of public opinion, the repeatedly expressed concern of a number of responsible biologists, and an investigation of the subject by the Senate Subcommittee on Energy, Resources, and the Environment, headed by Senator Philip A. Hart, of Michigan, the government, on April 15, placed restrictions on the use of 2,4,5-T in this country. On the same date, David Packard, Deputy Secretary of Defense, announced that the use of 2,4,5-T for destroying crops and defoliating trails in Communist-controlled areas of South Vietnam would be discontinued "pending a more thorough evaluation" of the safety of the chemical. It has recently become known that all herbicidal-spraying operations in Vietnam have been suspended since Deputy Secretary Packard's announcement. However, it has also been made known that this suspension stems primarily from the exigencies of the Cambodian invasion and that the Department of Defense reserves the option of resuming such operations.

In the June 20 issue of *The New Yorker,* I discussed the ineffectual nature of the restrictions that the Administration had placed on the use of 2,4,5-T in this country and the consequent continuing dangers to public health. I would now like to discuss some further implications of our herbicidal warfare in Vietnam. Throughout the nine years in which the United States has waged this warfare, the Department of Defense has insisted that "the herbicides used are nontoxic and not dangerous to man or animal life." Unfortunately, this assurance was not based on scientifically established fact; the truth is that some twenty years after the development of 2,4,5-T, by the American chemical- and biological-warfare people during the Second World War, not a single study had ever been made of possible harmful effects of 2,4,5-T on the unborn. In 1966, the Bionetics Research Laboratories, of Bethesda, Maryland, operating under a contract with the National Cancer Institute to study the teratogenic, or fetus-deforming, effects of a number of industrial and pesticidal compounds, did adduce data showing that 2,4,5-T had marked teratogenic effects on experimental mice and rats, but this information did not become public until late last year, owing to dilatoriness on the part of government agencies and a general reluctance on the part of members of the Administration, including the President's own science advisers, to inform the public forthrightly of the potential dangers. And after this information was forced out of the Administration, spokesmen for the Department of Defense continued up to mid-April of this year to insist that the use of 2,4,5-T in Vietnam presented no potential hazards to human health. At that time, the Surgeon General of the United States conceded before the Hart subcommittee that 2,4,5-T did indeed present enough of a hazard to women of childbearing age to warrant suspension of its use around homes and gardens.

At the time the Department of Defense announced its suspension of the use of 2,4,5-T, the American military had sprayed from the air onto the countryside and the inhabitants of Vietnam a total of at least 20,000 tons of the compound. There, 2,4,5-T has been used principally in a formulation, bearing the designation Agent Orange, that is an equal mixture of 2,4,5-T and 2,4-D. The latter has also never been shown to be nonhazardous to the unborn. Last year, a report summarizing the results of the same Bionetics Laboratories study that showed 2,4,5-T to be teratogenic characterized 2,4-D as "potentially dangerous" and "needing further study" as to teratogenicity. Since that time, another study, conducted by the Food and Drug Administration and using a formulation of 2,4-D on pregnant golden hamsters, is reported to have revealed teratogenic effects. The Surgeon General has said that he is not convinced that this study is conclusive evidence. However, another study within the F.D.A. has shown 2,4-D to have strong teratogenic effects on chick embryos.

If it is confirmed that 2,4-D poses dangers similar to those of 2,4,5-T, the American military will have unloaded not just 20,000 but 40,000 tons of teratogenic chemicals upon the Vietnamese countryside. The suspension of the use of 2,4,5-T in Vietnam has led to the suspension of the use of Agent Orange, and the Defense Department has consequently curtailed its defoliation operations—for the time being. According to a Department of Defense spokesman I talked with last week, the department is now compiling a report on the incidence of birth defects in South Vietnam to determine whether any of these can be connected with defoliation operations. I do not know what the findings of this survey will be, but it seems to me most improbable that, in the midst of all the chaos, disease, malnutrition, and various dislocations of war, any really accurate statistics concerning the causes of birth defects can be obtained. Certainly even in the United States, the compilation of reliable statistics on birth defects and their causes is very inadequate; that the American military can make an accurate survey in Vietnam, where reliable statistics on birth defects are virtually nonexistent, seems more than dubious.

The history of herbicidal warfare in Vietnam is the history of a program that quickly overwhelmed its original, limited objectives, took on a life of its own, and grew into a thing of devouring and destructive proportions. Putting an end to such a program obviously runs counter to many special military and economic interests. The sales representatives of the great chemical companies have been extremely active during the expanding herbicidal-warfare program in Vietnam; when the demand for 2,4,5-T and Agent Orange there reached its peak, it exceeded the available supply, and the companies were ready to propose alternatives. The military requirements in respect to 2,4,5-T in Vietnam grew from 200,000 gallons in 1965 to 1,300,000 gallons in 1966, and to three million gallons in 1967—requirements that far exceeded the output. While that was happening, the management of the Dow Chemical Company, one of the largest manufacturers of 2,4,5-T, sent representatives to Vietnam to confer with the military on ways of supplementing the 2,4,5-T, and apparently they agreed on an alternative to Agent Orange consisting of 2,4-D and a herbicide called picloram—a mixture that Dow was selling under the trade name of Tordon. Without any significant field tests in Vietnam, very large quantities of the 2,4-D and picloram mixture were sent out from the Dow factories in 1966 and 1967 and were put into use as a defoliant under the code name Agent White. (Dow was, and still is, its sole producer.) Now, picloram is one of the most persistent and long-lived of all herbicides. An article in a Dow publication on tests of the material in California reported that only three and a half per cent of it disappeared from certain clay soils after a period of 467 days. In this country, the use of picloram on food crops is not permitted; four Department of Agriculture scientists warned in a recent scientific paper, "Minute amounts of this potent herbicide irrigated on sensitive crops could have disastrous results." A spray operation using picloram to defoliate sections of the border between Canada and the United States, which our government started in 1966, was recently discontinued. It appears that even scientists working for the Army at Fort Detrick, Maryland, its research center for chemical and biological warfare, were not happy about the use of picloram in Vietnam, and in 1968, after production of Agent

Orange picked up, the use of Agent White dropped off sharply.

Considering this situation, in which the military, abetted by solicitous chemical salesmen, willingly supplemented the whole-sale use of one incompletely tested chemical with the wholesale use of another incompletely tested chemical, it seems proper to wonder whether the military might be considering the reintro-duction of picloram into defoliation operations in Vietnam. In this connection, it is hardly reassuring to learn of a communi-cation this month from a Dow vice-president to Senator Hart's subcommittee revealing that there has been recent discussion between Dow and the Defense Department about further pro-curement of Agent White for Vietnam.

Agent Orange and Agent White have been used primarily, though not exclusively, for forest defoliation in Vietnam. Mean-while, for crop destruction there, the military have primarily used Agent Blue, an aqueous solution of cacodylic acid. Since 1962, approximately half a million acres of crops, mostly rice, have been deliberately destroyed from the air in a "food-denial program," designed to deprive the Vietcong of rations. Accord-ing to pronouncements by American military spokesmen, these operations have been carried out only in "thinly populated" and "remote" areas "known to be used to produce food for Viet-cong military units." In terms of depriving Vietcong units in the affected areas of food, and thus reducing their military efficiency, the operations have been publicly characterized by the military as successful. However, I believe that the notion that the principal losers as a result of the program are the Vietcong is a fallacious one. The principal losers are members of the civilian population within and around the sprayed areas. If one takes the total figure of 500,000 acres of crops destroyed in Vietnam to represent rice crops, as it mainly does, it is pos-sible, on the basis of the average yield of rice per acre, to cal-culate that about 200,000 tons of growing rice have been de-stroyed so far. Three-quarters of what the Vietnamese people eat is rice, and, on the average, a Vietnamese consumes about 500 grams of rice a day, for a total of about one-fifth of a ton per year. Assuming that people in the affected areas have been practicing subsistence agriculture, one can calculate that the spraying of half a million acres would destroy enough rice to feed a million people for a year. Of those people, how many were Vietcong? If one accepts the Defense Department's claim that the affected areas are "thinly populated," one has to assume that the Department is calculating this population density in terms of a broad area. In terms of broad areas, the average Vietcong population is about two per cent of the total Vietnamese civilian population. Thus, it can be estimated that the American military destroyed the rice supply of a million people with the aim of denying food to 20,000 Vietcong. Or, to put it another way, in order to deprive the Vietcong of one ton of rice the American military has to destroy fifty tons of rice that would ordinarily support members of the civilian population. Yet if you deprive a million Vietnamese civilians of food in order to deprive 20,000 Vietcong of food, does it follow that the Vietcong *are* in fact deprived of food? It seems that occasionally local Vietcong units have indeed suffered food shortages, but prisoner-of-war reports indicate that on the whole the Vietcong have continued to be adequately fed, crop destruction or no crop destruction. In the history of warfare, as many competent biologists and nutritionists—including the well-known Professor Jean Mayer of Harvard, who is President Nixon's special adviser on nutrition—have pointed out, it has always been the fighting men who had first claim to whatever food was available, and it has been the civilians who suffered the shortages. Guerrilla war in Vietnam is no exception to this rule, and the fact seems to be that, as a whole, the crop-destruction program has not achieved its purpose. At least a million people have been denied the equivalent of a year's supply of food, and at least a million gallons of a solution of cacodylic acid, which is fifty-four per cent arsenic, and is described in the authoritative "Merck Index" as "poisonous," has been sprayed on a country we are supposedly defending. The Department of Defense has always insisted that the formulation of cacodylic acid that is used in Vietnam is harmless to men and animals alike. However, the

Defense Department for years gave us the same kind of assurance about 2,4,5-T without ever having initiated the necessary tests for teratogenic, mutagenic, or carcinogenic effects to determine if in fact it was harmless. A military document known as Combined Campaign Plan, Joint U.S. Psychological Warfare Directive, instructs personnel:

> In defoliation operations, explain the necessity for the operation, explain the effect of the chemicals with emphasis on the fact that they are not toxic to human beings or animals, explain the indemnification program, and encourage the people to become refugees and leave the area that is to become permanently defoliated.

An official in the Pentagon who is connected with the herbicidal program recently told a visitor that pilots carrying out American herbicidal-spraying missions "hate" Agent Blue, because "it takes the paint off their planes" and has a generally corrosive effect. As the Pentagon sees it, apparently, Agent Blue is not toxic to men or to animals; it is toxic only to airplanes.

While the military may have officially expressed the opinion that the defoliation and crop-destruction operations in Vietnam have been successful, the private views of many people connected with the programs there are not nearly so positive. I have heard it reported by people close to the operations that as far back as 1967, at the peak of the crop-destruction program, internal reviews made by the military indicated that the primary effect was upon civilians, and that the operations did not affect the military power of the Vietcong to any substantial degree. At least certain civilian employees of the Pentagon seem to have been made aware, by prisoner-of-war and other reports, of the extreme bitterness that the defoliation and crop-destruction operations have engendered among the Vietnamese peasants, whose rice crops, growing on their ancestral ground, represent their lifework, their security, and their hopes. This bitterness has undoubtedly contributed to the successful recruitment of civilians to the Vietcong cause, and therefore one sees that quite a few of the Vietcong whom the American military have tried unsuccessfully to starve out are likely to be replaced thanks to the "food-denial program." Very recently, a responsible civilian in the Pentagon with whom I talked about herbicidal warfare began to wonder out loud whether, in view of all the difficulties involved, the game, as he put it, was really worth the candle. Yet the urge to go on with the game, if that is the word, remains. The Defense Department contemplates further crop-destruction sorties after the pullout of American forces from Cambodia. "We're just now getting into some harvesting times," a military source in Saigon was quoted as saying in the *Times* of June 23.

The last thing the people responsible for herbicidal warfare are willing to say is that the program should be stopped altogether. They do understand the value of appearing to give ground to critics. But one of the military men in charge of the entire herbicidal-warfare program in Vietnam is reliably reported to have told a visitor some time ago that he didn't really know how effective the program was but that he thought the fact of its existence would help the cause of the chemical-warfare people in the Army. As a man who is very familiar with the program in Vietnam told me recently, "What's going on now is that as the pullout from Vietnam continues, the people in charge of different weapons systems are struggling among themselves for a piece of the postwar pie. There's intense competition over the question of what programs are going to survive. This includes the herbicidal-program people. They are ready enough to curtail their operations now just so long as they can keep the program somehow ticking over and keep the principle alive."

It seems to me that not only the program but the principle should be killed off. It seems to me that the nine-year disaster of herbicidal warfare in Vietnam can and should be ended now by the force of public opinion. The manner in which the employment of hazardous and untested chemical herbicides in Vietnam has grown, feeding on itself, and inflicting suffering, hardship, and the risk of damage to the unborn upon the Vietnamese population, brings it altogether too close to the monstrous vision of full-scale chemical and biological warfare.

Last November, President Nixon proclaimed that the United States was renouncing the first use of lethal or incapacitating chemical weapons, and that under no circumstances, even in retaliation, would it use biological weapons. He also announced that he was submitting to the Senate for ratification the Geneva Protocol of 1925, which prohibits the use of chemical and biological weapons in warfare. The President did not include chemical defoliants and crop-destroying agents among weapons we renounce. I believe that the time has come for the President to put a formal end to herbicidal warfare, in Vietnam now and anywhere else in the future, and for our government to make it clear that the United States regards herbicidal-warfare agents as banned weapons under the Geneva Protocol.

Although the Protocol, which was drawn up before the invention of chemical defoliants and crop-destroying agents, does not specifically mention herbicides, it is known to have been deliberately written in broad language in order to include in its prohibitions a wide spectrum of noxious warfare agents. Last winter, a resolution holding that the Geneva Protocol prohibits the use in war of all chemical agents directed at men, animals, or plants was introduced at the United Nations General Assembly by Sweden and twenty other nations, and although the United States voted against it and brought pressure on many other delegations to do likewise, the resolution was passed by a vote of eighty to three.

In a letter to the *Times* in December, 1969, Philip Noel-Baker recalled a conversation he had had with Henri Bonnet, who, like Mr. Noel-Baker, served in the League of Nations Secretariat. According to Mr. Noel-Baker, M. Bonnet assured him, "The form of words [in the Protocol] is good. It prohibits every kind of chemical or bacterial weapon that anyone could possibly devise. And it has to. Perhaps someday a criminal lunatic might invent some devilish thing that would destroy animals and crops."

APPENDICES

REPORT OF THE SECRETARY'S COMMISSION ON PESTICIDES AND THEIR RELATIONSHIP TO ENVIRONMENTAL HEALTH

(U.S. Department of Health, Education, and Welfare, December 1969)

TERATOGENICITY OF PESTICIDES

Summary and Conclusions

Teratology deals with the etiology and development of congenital malformations. Congenital malformations are generally defined as gross structural abnormalities of prenatal origin, present at birth or manifesting shortly after, which kill or disable. In a broader sense, teratogenesis is considered to include histological, biochemical, and functional abnormalities of prenatal origin.

Congenital malformations present obvious personal, medical, and social stresses. Additionally, it has been recently estimated that the costs to society of one severely malformed child, in terms of medical and other care and deprivation of potential earnings, amount to several hundred thousand dollars.

There are now well over 400 substances that, in various forms and combinations, are currently used as pesticides. Pesticides may represent an important potential teratogenic hazard. Therefore any teratogenic pesticide to which the population is exposed should be promptly identified so that appropriate precautions can be taken to revent risk of human exposure. It is feasible to test these substances for teratogenic effects in test animals so that potential hazards to human health can be evaluated.

For these and other reasons detailed in the report, we conclude that:

a. All currently used pesticides should be tested for teratogenicity in the near future in 2 or more mammalian species chosen on the basis of the closest metabolic and pharmacologic similarity to human beings possible. Pesticides should be tested at various concentrations including levels substantially higher than those to which the human population are likely to be exposed. Test procedures should also reflect routes related to human exposure. Apart from the obvious route of ingestion, attention should be directed to other routes of exposure, including inhalation exposures from pesticide aerosols and vaporizing pesticide strips used domestically and exposures from skin absorption. Parenteral administration is an appropriate test route for pesticides to which humans are exposed by inhalation, or for pesticides which are systemically absorbed following ingestion.

b. The use of currently registered pesticides to which humans are exposed and which are found to be teratogenic by suitable test procedures in one or more mammalian species should be immediately restricted to prevent risk of human exposure. Such pesticides, in current use, include Captan, Carbaryl; the butyl, isopropyl, and isooctyl esters of 2,4-D Folpet; mercurials; PCNB; and 2,4,5-T. The teratogenicity of 2,4-D, the other salts and esters of both 2,4-D and 2,4,5-T, and that of IPC should be investigated further.

c. Pesticides found to be inactive after appropriate testing can be considered as provisionally safe, unless other evidence of teratogenicity develops.

d. No new pesticide should be registered until tested for teratogenicity by suitable procedures. Any pesticide found to be teratogenic should only be used in circumstances where risk of human exposure is minimal.

e. Efforts should be made to improve and standardize procedures for teratogenicity testing and population monitoring. A scientific group or commission should be charged with responsibility for continued surveillance of the whole problem of pesticide teratogenesis.

Methodologies for Teratogenicity Testing

Introduction

Prior to 1963, the Food and Drug Administration did not require evaluation of teratogenicity. As a result of the thalidomide disaster, the need for data on teratogenicity became evident. In 1963, the President's Science Advisory Committee on "Use of Pesticides" recommended that toxicity studies on pesticides include effects on reproduction through at least 2 generations in at least 2 species of warm-blooded animals. Observations to be included were effects on fertility, size and weight of litters, fetal mortality, teratogenicity, and growth and development of sucklings and weanlings. Such toxicity studies including the three-generation procedure were not designed primarily to detect teratogenicity and thus may not be appropriate.

The potential teratogenicity of chemicals may be detected by two complementary approaches. First, chemicals or other agents may be administered to experimental animals to determine whether they induce prenatal damage. Secondly, and on a *post hoc* basis, human populations may be epidemiologically surveyed to detect greographical or temporal clusters of unusual types or frequencies of congenital malformations. Combinations of these approaches are likely to ensure early detection and identification of teratogenic hazards.

Experimentally, a complex of factors are needed to elicit teratogenic effects. These relate to gestation period, genotype of the pregnant animals, dosage, mode of administration and metabolic transformation of teratogen. For example, teratogens may be effective only at a certain dose range, whether high or low, narrow or wide, below which development is apparently undisturbed, and above which death *in utero* results.

Most agents are teratogenic only in the developmentally labile early period of gestation, during which active organogenesis occurs. In humans, this sensitive period extends approximately from the end of the first week of pregnancy to the 12th week. Other circumstances may also influence the effectiveness of human teratogens, such as maternal nutritional, demographic, socioeconomic, and cultural factors, physiological states, and temporal and seasonal situations. Thus a potential teratogen may manifest its effect only when particular conditions conjoin.

The relationship between human exposure to a teratogen and subsequent induction of congenital abnormalities is generally not obvious. Any one teratogen may produce a multiplicity of effects and any specific effect may be produced by various teratogens. In test animals, the teratogenic response may differ from species to species. In humans, differences in genetic, metabolic, and environmental influences may contribute to a variety of specific effects from exposure to a particular teratogenic agent. Induced and spontaneous effects may be difficult to distinguish. The teratogenicity of thalidomide might have been missed had it not produced malformations rarely encountered; additionally, only a fraction of the pregnant women who took thalidomide had defective children.

Consequently, further data on the possible teratogenic effects of pesticides in experimental animals are urgently needed to provide a basis for evaluating potential hazards to human health. . . .

Literature Review

Bionetics animal studies

Bionetics Research Laboratories of Litton Industries, during 1965–68 under a contract for the National Cancer Institute (NCI Contracts PH 43–64–57 and PH 43–67–735), tested various pesticides and related compounds for teratogenic effects. These studies were designed as large-scale screening tests. The Bionetics data were re-analyzed statistically to account for litter effects. The results of this statistical re-evaluation are presented in this section. More detailed material on these pesticides will be published in the future.

a. *Summary of findings from Bionetics animal studies.* Tested more extensively than other pesticides, 2,4,5-T was clearly teratogenic as evidenced by production of statistically increased proportions of litters affected, and increased proportions of abnormal fetuses within litters in both DMSO and honey for both C57BL/6 and AKR mice. In particular, cleft palate and cystic kidneys were significantly more prevalent. In addition, a hybrid strain resulting from a C57BL/6 female and AKR male showed significant increases in anomalies, in particular cystic kidney, when administered at 113 mg./kg. of body weight in DMSO.

Additionally, 2,4,5-T was tested in Sprague-Dawley rats. When given orally at dosages of 4.6, 10.0 and 46.4 mg./kg. on days 10 through 15 of gestation, an excessive fetal mortality, up to 60 percent at the highest dose, and high incidence of abnormalities in the survivors was obtained. The incidence of fetuses with kidney anomalies was three-fold that of the controls, even with the smallest dosage tested.

PCNB produced an increase in renal agenesis between litters, and within litters, when administered orally from days 6–14 or days 6–10 of pregnancy. However, renal agenesis was not produced when PCNB was administered only from days 10–14 of pregnancy. These effects were produced in only the C57BL/6 strain of mice.

Other pesticides producing a statistically significant increase in the proportion of litters containing abnormal fetuses and in the increased incidence of abnormal fetuses within litters were: Captan, Folpet, 2,4-D isooctyl ester, 2,4-D butyl ester, 2,4-D isopropyl ester, carbaryl (Sevin), and IPC. . . . The results for carbaryl and for IPC were less consistent than for other compounds. (The pesticides 2,4,5-T, PCNB, Captan, Folpet, Carbaryl, IPC, and the butyl and isopropyl esters of 2,4-D were statistically significant at the .01 level, for one or more tests. This criterion is similar to that adopted by the Technical Panel on Carcinogenesis, Chapter 5, to identify "positive" compounds. The isooctyl ester of 2,4-D was significant at the 0.05 level.)

Compounds inducing only an increase in the proportion of abnormal fetuses within litters were: α-naphthol, and 2,4-D methyl ester. The statistical significance of these results was relatively weak; further study is required before any conclusions can be reached. Similarly, 2,4-D produced only an increase in the proportion of abnormal litters during 1965 in AKR mice. Due to the teratogenic activity of certain of its esters, 2,4-D should be studied further.

Carbaryl plus piperonyl butoxide did not show an overall increase in nonspecific anomalies, but resulted in significantly more cystic kidneys for doses above 10 mg./kg. carbaryl plus 100 μl./kg. piperonyl butoxide.

It must be emphasized that failure to detect statistically significant increases of anomalies may be due to insensitivity resulting from experimental variation and small numbers of litters tested. In addition, higher fetal mortality among some of the "negative" compounds may be selectively eliminating abnormal fetuses.

b. Methods. Four strains of mice were used: C57BL/6, AKR, C3H, and A/Ha. Most of the studies were performed with the C57BL/6 strain. A hybrid fetus resulting from mating a C57BL/6 female with an AKR male was used to study a few compounds. More restricted studies were also made on Sprague-Dawley rats; results of these with reference to 2,4,5-T are considered separately.

Most compounds were administered subcutaneously in 0.1 ml. solutions of dimethylsulfoxide (DMSO). Water soluble compounds were administered in saline, and sometimes also in DMSO. Compounds administered orally were given by gavage in 0.1 ml. in a 50-percent honey solution. Groups of positive controls and untreated controls were included, as well as controls receiving only DMSO, saline, or honey. While controls were run periodically throughout the duration of the study, compounds and controls were not matched with respect to either route or date of administration.

Virgin females were used in these studies. The onset of pregnancy was determined by detection of vaginal plugs. Compounds were administered daily from the sixth to the 14th day of pregnancy (15th day for AKR mice). Mice were sacrificed on the 18th day (19th day for AKR mice) of gestation. On sacrifice, fetuses were examined for anomalies. Approximately two-thirds of the fetuses were then stored in Bouin's solution until necropsy. Remaining fetuses were stained with alizarin red S after proper processing. Numbers of resorption sites and dead fetuses were also scored.

c. Statistical analysis. All analyses were performed on a *per* litter basis rather than a *per* fetus basis, since initial investigation indicated that the occurrences of anomalies among fetuses within litters were correlated. The large litter-to-litter variation may reflect some maternal effect, an indication of the effective dose level of the compound actually reaching the fetuses, experimental variation, or, as is most likely, some combination of the three factors.

While there were no statistically significant time trends within the various control groups in terms of the onset of fetal anomalies in the C57BL/6 mice, the incidence of fetal mortality was certainly time-dependent in this strain, with 1965 being characterized by a low incidence of prenatal deaths. Furthermore, there was a period of approximately 6 months, extending from the latter part of 1965 into early 1966, during which no control animals were tested. During this period a change in the substrain of C57BL/6 mice used in the study took place. Finally, among abnormal litters, as defined by litters containing at least one abnormal fetus, there was some suggestion that the distribution of abnormal fetuses *per* litter was stochastically larger in the DMSO controls than it was in the untreated controls. Thus, the possibility exists of a time/strain/ solvent interaction that is undetectable in the controls because the level of background teratologic activity is relatively low. This potential interaction effect could either enhance or dissipate the effect of any given compound, depending on the conditions under which it was administered. Thus, the data were necessarily separated by both time period and solvent for the purposes of analysis. Similarly, an increase in fetal anomalies in the DMSO controls of the AKR mice was noted after November 1966. Thus, the AKR data were analyzed separately in two time periods.

It should be noted that not all compounds were administered on more than one occasion or in more than one solvent or strain. Thus, in general the compounds in the study cannot be compared for teratogenic potential, since those that were tested extensively were more likely to show some adverse effect and, perhaps, less likely to appear consistent over time, solvent, and/or strain.

As noted, approximately two-thirds of the fetuses were stored in Bouin's solution until necropsied; the remainder being stained with alizarin red. However, in many instances the proportion of necropsied fetuses was slightly higher for the compound under investigation than for the corresponding controls. It is doubtful if this discrepancy could have any appreciable effect on the conclusions since the incidence of anomalies detectable only by necropsy among control animals was relatively low. Furthermore, if all of the control and test mice had been necropsied, the significance of the differences observed in this study would be intensified. Thus, no effort was made to correct for inequalities in the necropsy/stain ratio in the present analysis. Additionally, no attempt was made to correct for differences in litter sizes or sex-ratios within litters, since both of these factors may, at least in part, reflect effects of the compound under test.

d. Results. Data for pesticides yielding a statistically increased level of anomalies in C57BL/6 and AKR mice are listed in tables 1 and 2, respectively. The proportion of abnormal litters gives the proportion of litters containing one or more abnormal fetuses, as a measure of the prevalence of anomalies across litters. The proportion of abnormal fetuses *per* litter gives a measure of the prevalence of anomalies within litters. The proportion of abnormal fetuses *per* litter for litters containing abnormal fetuses gives a measure of the prevalence of anomalies within affected litters. A significant increase of dead fetuses and resorptions is also listed. Some tests were conducted on only one particular day or on adjacent days as listed. Eye anomalies, mainly microphthalmia and anophthalmia, accounted for approximately 50 percent of the individual anomalies in C57BL/6 mice. To a large extent, results in table 1 reflect changes in the incidence of eye anomalies. Yet, when the data were analyzed excluding fetuses with microphthalmia only, there were no striking changes in the results. In the last column of table 1, statistically significant increase in various types of anomalies other than eye anomalies are listed. The positive controls, trypan blue and ethyleneimine, table 1, and 6-aminonicotinamide, table 2, showed elevated levels of anomalies, although the latter control did not yield consistent results over all dose levels.

Only those test conditions which resulted in statistically elevated incidences of anomalies are listed in tables 1 and 2. Some compounds gave no increase in anomalies (based on the overall incidence if tested in both time periods) when tested in other solvents, strains, or dose levels (table 3). It must be emphasized that failure to detect a statistically significant increase in anomalies may only be a reflection of experimental insensitivity due to experimental and biological variation and insufficient number of litters. Thus, compounds showing no increases cannot be considered nonteratogenic. For example, trypan blue in DMSO at the highest dose level tested, 37.5 mg./kg., did not show an increase in anomalies, possibly due to higher fetal mortality. Standard corrected 2×2 chi-square tests were used to compare the proportion of abnormal litters for the compound with the controls in the same solvent. In the cases where tests were conducted in two time periods, the results from the two chi-squares were combined. The levels of statistical significance for the combined tests are listed under the total column for proportion of abnormal litters.

The distribution of the proportion of abnormal fetuses per litter (tables 1 and 2) for compounds were compared with the

TABLE 1. TESTS WHICH DISPLAYED SIGNIFICAN·

Compound	Solvent	Dose per kg of body weight	Proportion of abnormal litters			Proportion of abnormal fetuses per litter		
			1965	1966–68	Total	1965	1966–68	Total
Negative controls:								
Untreated	None		.42	.39	.40	.08	.11	.10
Controls	DMSO		.53	.41	.46	.16	.12	.13
Do	Saline		.52	.37	.43	.13	.10	.11
Do	Honey			.47	.47		.15	.15
Positive controls:								
Trypan blue	DMSO	5.0 mg	.60		.60	.32		.32
Do	DMSO	12.5 mg	.86		.86	.44***		.44***
Do	DMSO	37.5 mg	.60		.60	.36		.36
Do	Saline	5.0 mg	1.00		1.00	.61***		.61***
Do	do	12.5 mg	.71		.71	.49**		.49**
Do	do	37.5 mg	.71		.71	.33*		.33*
Ethyleneimine	do	4.64 µl	1.00*		1.00*	.49***		.49***
Experimental:								
2,4,5-T	DMSO	113 mg		.79**	.79**		.56***	.56**
2,4,5-T	Honey	46.4 mg		1.00*	1.00*		.37**	.37**
2,4,5-T	do	113 mg		1.00**	1.00**		.70***	.70**
PCNB (days 6–14)	do	215 mg		.88*	.88*		.25**	.25**
PCNB (days 6–14)	do	464 mg		.67 ⎱**	.67 ⎱**		.25 ⎱***	.25 ⎱
PCNB (days 6–10)	do	464 mg		1.00 ⎰	1.00 ⎰		.38 ⎰	.38 ⎰
Captan	DMSO	100 mg	1.00*	.61	.71***	.58***	.27	.35**
Folpet	DMSO	100 mg		.77**	.77**		.29***	.29**
2,4-D Isooctyl ester	DMSO	48 µl	1.00*		1.00*	.24		.24
2,4-D Isooctyl ester	DMSO	130 µl		.67	.67		.28**	.28**
2,4-D Butyl ester	DMSO	100 µl		.75**	.75**		.25***	.25**
2,4-D Isopropyl ester	DMSO	94 µl		.70**	.70**		.26***	.26**
Carbaryl	DMSO	100 mg	1.00*	.54	.71**	.46***	.16	.26**
IPC	DMSO	850 mg	1.00**	.43	.71*	.46***	.09	.27**
α-Naphthol	DMSO	10 mg	.86		.86	.33*		.39*
2,4-D Methyl ester	DMSO	106 mg		.83	.83		.30*	.30*
Carbaryl+Piperonyl Butoxide	DMSO 10 mg+ 100 µl			.50	.50		.13	.13
Do	DMSO 46.4 mg + 464 µl			.50	.50		.10	.10

Significance level: *(.10). **(.05). ***(.01).

NCREASES OF ANOMALIES (*C57BL/6 mice*)

Proportion of abnormal fetuses per litter in abnormal litters			Increased mortality	Tests repeated over time	No. of live litters		Increased anomalies other than eye
965	1966–68	Total			1965	1966–68	
8	.28	.25			26	69	
3	.28	.29			70	112	
4	.28	.26			31	46	
	.32	.32				32	
4		.54	Yes		5		⎫
2**		.52**	Yes		7		⎬ Hydrocephaly
0		.60	Yes		5		⎭
1**		.61**			5		
9***		.69***	Yes		7		
6**		.46**	Yes		7		Hydrocephaly
9***		.49***	Yes	No	7		
	.71***	.71***	Yes		14		Cleft palate, cystic kidney
	.37	.37		No	6		
	.70***	.70***	Yes		9		Cleft palate, cystic kidney
	.29	.29		No	8		⎫
	.38	.38			12		⎬ Renal agenesis
	.37	.37		No	10		⎭
8**	.44	.49**	Yes		6	18	
	.38*	.38*				13	
4		.24			6		
	.41*	.41*				16	
	.33	.33				30	Agnathia
	.37*	.37*				20	
5*	.29	.37			6	11	Hydrocephaly, skeletal
5*		.46*			7	7	
8		.38			7		
	.36	.36				6	
	.26	.26		No		6	⎫ Cystic kidney
	.21	.21				12	⎭

TABLE 2.   TESTS WHICH DISPLAYED SIGNIFICAN

Compound	Solvent	Dose per kg of body weight	Proportion of abnormal litters			Proportion of abnorma fetuses per litter		
			†11/66	12/66††	Total	†11/66	12/66††	Total
Negative controls:								
Control	DMSO		.05	.37	.21	.01	.06	.03
Do	Honey			.00	.00		.00	.00
Positive controls:								
6-amino-nicotina-mide	DMSO	34 mg	.56***		.56***	.31**		.31**
6-amino-nicotina-mide (1)	DMSO	68 mg	.00		.00	.00		.00
Experimental:								
2,4,5-T	DMSO	113 mg	.50***	1.00**	.71***	.20**	.40***	.29**
2,4,5-T	Honey	113 mg		1.00***	1.00***		.54***	.54**
2,4-D	DMSO	98 mg	.43**	.29	.36*	.12	.05	.08

*Significance Level .10. **Significance Level .05. ***Significance Level .01. †Through 11/66. ††After 11/66.
Note: (1) With the .68 mg/kg dose, as compared to the .34 mg/kg dose, fewer implantations and a higher fetal mortality were encountered, resulting in fewer live fetuses per litter.

appropriate control distribution by use of the nonparametric Mann-Whitney U-test. This test requires that the proportion of abnormal fetuses per litter is independent from litter to litter, but requires no assumption about the frequency distribution of these proportions. Again, where litters were run in both time periods, the significance level for the combined tests is given under the total column. Bracketed data include groups which were combined before statistical tests were conducted.

NCREASES OF ANOMALIES (*AKR mice*)

Proportion of abnormal fetuses per litter in abnormal litters			Increased mortality	Tests repeated over time	No. of live litters		Special anomalies
11/66	12/66††	Total			†11/66	12/66††	
1	.16	.15			37	35	
						12	
55		.55			9		Cleft palate
					7		
0*	.40**	.40*			8	6	Cleft palate
	.54	.54	yes			6	Cleft palate
8	.16	.23			7	7	

EXCERPTS FROM THE BIONETICS LABORATORIES REPORT

From Volume III
Evaluation of the Teratogenic Activity of
Selected Pesticides and Industrial
Chemicals in Mice & Rats

———

2,4,5-T—BRL NO. 061

(Table A-22 Original Bionetics Report)

This compound was given by the oral route to BL6 mice at dosages of 46.4 and 113 mg/kg and to AKR mice at 113 mg/kg. It was given by subcutaneous injection to BL6 mice at dosages of 21.5 and 113 mg/kg and to AKR mice and B6AK hybrids at 113 mg/kg. It was also given subcutaneously to C3H mice at 215 mg/kg, but there were too few of these to merit inclusion in the discussion which follows. Administration was for eight days (6th through 14th) in most cases; for nine days (6th through 15th) in some; and for five days (10th through 14th) in one case—the details are indicated in the tabulated results. Subcutaneous administration used DMSO as a vehicle; oral used 50% honey.

With the single exception of the lowest dosage used (21.5 mg/kg to BL6 subcutaneously) all dosages, routes, and strains resulted in increased incidence of abnormal fetuses. The incidence of cleft palate was high at the 113 mg/kg dosage, but not at lower levels. The incidence of cystic kidney was also high except in the AKR strain and in the BL6 mice which received 46.4 mg/kg orally. Fetal mortality was increased in all groups given 113 mg/kg for eight or nine days, but not in mice (BL6) given this dosage for only five days nor in the two groups of BL6 mice given lesser dosages (46.4 mg/kg orally and 21.5 mg/kg subcutaneously).

Most fetal and maternal measurements showed inconsistent changes from which no conclusions can be drawn. In contrast there was a highly consistent decrease in maternal weight gain in BL6 mice given 113 mg/kg by either route. Lower dosages and the AKR strain showed either no change or a slight increase. All dosages, strains, and routes showed an increase in the maternal liver weight and this led to a further study discussed separately below.

These results imply a hazard of teratogenesis in the use of this compound. The problems of extrapolation preclude definition of the hazard on the basis of these studies, but its existence seems clear.

Liver Weight Study (Table A-22)

The observed influence of 2,4,5-T on maternal liver weight as mentioned above raised a question as to its effect on the fetal liver. This was answered by a study carried out in BL6 mice using subcutaneous injections of DMSO solutions at a dosage of 113 mg/kg only. The period of administration was lengthened to cover the period from the 9th through 17th day of gestation. Separate control groups were used concurrently. Except for the inclusion of fetal liver weight, measurements were made as previously described.

The fetal livers of the 2,4,5-T treated mice weighed significantly more than those of controls given DMSO only and the weights of the whole fetuses were significantly less. Correspondingly, there was an increase in the fetal liver weight expressed as percent of body weight.

Other observations were consistent with those reported above. The incidence of abnormal fetuses was unusually high as were those of cleft palate and cystic kidney.

Rats—Sprague-Dawley Strain (Table A-22)

Because of the potential importance of the findings in mice, an additional study was carried out in rats of the Sprague-Dawley strain. Using dosages of 21.5 and 46.4 mg/kg suspended in honey and given by the oral route on the 6th through 15th days of gestation, we observed excessive fetal mortality (almost 80%) and a high incidence of abnormalities in the survivors. When the beginning of administration was delayed until the 10th day, fetal mortality was somewhat less, but still quite high even when dosage was reduced to 4.6 mg/kg. The incidence of abnormal fetuses was threefold that in controls even with the smallest dosage and shortest period used. Fetal and maternal measurements showed only occasional instances of significant differences from controls except in the case of maternal liver weight which was consistently increased in all 2,4,5-T treated animals.

It seems inescapable that 2,4,5-T is teratogenic in this strain of rats when given orally at the dosage schedules used here. These findings lend emphasis to the hazard implied by the results of studies on mice.

RAT STUDY OF THE SPRAGUE-DAWLEY STRAIN

Compound	Non-Treated	Honey	Honey	2,4,5-T	2,4,5-T	2,4,5-T	2,4,5-T	2,4,5-T	2,4,5-T
Strain Sprague-Dawley									
Dosage mg/kg		200†	200†	4.6	10.0	21.5	21.5	46.4	46.4
Vehicle/Route		Honey/po	Honey/po	Honey/po	Honey/po	Honey/po	Honey/po	Honey/po	Honey
Administration Days Gestation		10–15	6–15	10–15	10–15	10–15	6–15	10–15	6–15
No. Litters	7	14	6	8	7	3	4	6	2
Total No. Fetuses	69	122	46	66	50	20	12	16	4
Percent abnormal fetuses									
Total	10	13	7	39	78	90	92	100	75
P	—	0.5	0.9	0.001	0.001	0.001	—	—	—
With renal anomalies	10	13	6	36	46	55	42	50	25
Anomalies No. observed									
Renal									
Enlarged pelvis	7	16	3	16	9	4	5	5	0
Cystic kidney	0	1	0	11	15	7	0	3	1
Cleft palate	0	0	0	0	0	0	0	0	1
Hemorrhagic GI tract	0	0	0	3	27	18	10	15	2

† μl/rat

EMPLOYMENT OF RIOT CONTROL AGENTS, FLAME, SMOKE, ANTIPLANT AGENTS, AND PERSONNEL DETECTORS IN COUNTERGUERRILLA OPERATIONS

Department of the Army Training Circular TC 3-16 April 1969

ANTIPLANT AGENT OPERATIONS

Section I
Technical Aspects

51. General. Antiplant agents are chemical agents which possess a high offensive potential for destroying or seriously limiting the production of food and defoliating vegetation. These compounds include herbicides that kill or inhibit the growth of plants; plant growth regulators that either regulate or inhibit plant growth, sometimes causing plant death; desiccants that dry up plant foliage; and soil sterilants that prevent or inhibit the growth of vegetation by action with the soil. Military applications for antiplant agents are based on denying the enemy food and concealment.

52. Antiplant Agents in Use.

a. ORANGE.

(1) *Description.* Agent ORANGE is the Standard A agent. It is composed of a 50:50 mixture of the n-butyl esters of 2,4-D and 2,4,5-T (app D and C1, TM 3-215). ORANGE appears as a dark-brown oily liquid which is insoluble in water but miscible in oils such as diesel fuel. It weighs about 10.75

pounds per gallon and becomes quite viscous as the temperature drops, solidifying at 45° F. It is noncorrosive, of low volatility, and nonexplosive, but deteriorates rubber.

(2) *Rate of application.* The recommended rate of application of ORANGE is 3 gallons per acre. This may vary depending on the type of vegetation (app C). In some situations better coverage may be obtained by diluting ORANGE with diesel fuel oil, which results in a less viscous solution that is dispersed in smaller droplets. Dilution may also be required when using dispersion equipment which does not permit the flow rate to be conveniently adjusted to 3 gallons per acre. See discussion of application methods in paragraphs 57 and 58.

(3) *Effect on foliage.* ORANGE penetrates the waxy covering of leaves and is absorbed into the plant system. It affects the growing points of the plant, resulting in its death. Rains occurring within the first hour after spraying will not reduce the effectiveness of ORANGE to the extent that they reduce the effectiveness of aqueous solutions. Broadleaf plants are highly susceptible to ORANGE. Some grasses can be controlled but require a much higher dose rate than broadleaf plants. Susceptible plants exhibit varying degrees of susceptibility to OR-ANGE. Death of a given plant may occur within a week or less, or may require up to several months depending on the plant's age, stage of growth, susceptibility, and the dose rate. See employment considerations in paragraphs 53 through 55.

(4) *Safety precautions and decontamination.* ORANGE is relatively nontoxic to man or animals. No injuries have been reported to personnel exposed to aircraft spray. Personnel subject to splashes from handling the agent need not be alarmed, but should shower and change clothes at a convenient opportunity. ORANGE is noncorrosive to metals but will remove aircraft paint and walkway coatings. Contaminated aircraft should be washed with soapy water to remove the agent. Rubber hoses and other rubber parts of transfer and dissemination equipment will deteriorate and require replacement, since OR-ANGE softens rubber.

b. BLUE (Phytar 560G).

(1) *Description.* Agent BLUE is an aqueous solution containing about 3 pounds per gallon of the sodium salt of cacodylic acid, the proper amount of surfactant (a substance which increases the effectiveness of the solution), and a neutralizer to prevent corrosion of metal spray apparatus. BLUE is the agent normally used for crop destruction.

(2) *Rate of application.* BLUE may be sprayed as received from the manufacturer without dilution, if desired. The recommended application rate for crop destruction is about 1 to 2 gallons per acre (app C). However, much higher use rates of BLUE are required to kill tall grasses, such as elephant grass or sugarcane, because of the large masses of vegetation. For hand-spray operations, two gallons of BLUE diluted with water to make 50 gallons will give a solution that can be dispersed by hand at a rate equivalent to approximately 1 to 3 gallons of pure agent per acre.

(3) *Effect on foliage.* Enough BLUE applied to any kind of foliage will cause it to dry and shrivel, but the agent is more effective against grassy plants than broadleaf varieties. Best results are obtained when the plant is thoroughly covered, since the agent kills by absorption of moisture from the leaves. The plants will die within 2 to 4 days or less and can then be burned if permitted to dry sufficiently. BLUE in low dose rates can also prevent grain formation in rice without any apparent external effect. The plant develops normally but does not yield a crop. Spray rates higher than about one-half gallon per acre usually kill the crop. Although BLUE can produce relatively rapid defoliation, regrowth may occur again in about 30 days. Repeated spraying is necessary to provide a high degree of continuous plant kill.

(4) *Safety precautions and decontamination.* Normal sanitary precautions should be followed when handling BLUE. Although it contains a form of arsenic, BLUE is relatively nontoxic. It should not be taken internally, however. Any material that gets on the hands, face, or other parts of the body should be washed off at the first opportunity. Clothes that become wet

with a solution of BLUE should be changed. Aircraft used for spraying this solution should be washed well afterward. When WHITE is added to BLUE, a precipitate forms that will clog the system. If the same spray apparatus is to be used for spraying agents WHITE and BLUE, the system must be flushed to assure that all residue of the previous agent is removed.

c. WHITE (Tordon 101).

(1) *Description.* The active ingredients of agent WHITE are 20 percent picloram and 80 percent isopropylamine salt of 2,4-D. Active ingredients constitute about 25 percent of the solution. A surfactant is also present. WHITE is soluble in water, noncorrosive, nonflammable, nonvolatile, immiscible in oils, and more viscous than ORANGE at the same temperature.

(2) *Rate of application.* WHITE usually should be applied at a rate of 3 to 5 gallons per acre on broadleaf vegetation. However, the rate may vary depending on the type of flora. Quantities required to control jungle vegetation may vary from 5 to 12 gallons per acre. This quantity exceeds the spray capability of most aircraft spray systems for a single pass. It is usually unfeasible in large-scale military operations to apply such large volumes. For ground-based spray operations, however, high volumes are necessary. Hand-spray operations cannot evenly cover a whole acre with only 3 gallons of solution. Three gallons of WHITE diluted to a 30-gallon solution can be more easily sprayed over an area of one acre. The manufacturer recommends diluting WHITE with sufficient water to make a 10-gallon solution for each gallon of agent.

(3) *Effect on foliage.* WHITE kills foliage in the same manner as ORANGE, since 80 percent of the active ingredient is 2,4-D. PICLORAM is more effective than 2,4-D, but acts slower. WHITE is effective on many plant species, and equal to or more effective than ORANGE on the more woody species. The material must be absorbed through the leaves. The water solution does not penetrate the waxy covering of leaves as well as oily mixtures and is more easily washed off by rain.

(4) *Safety precautions and decontamination.* WHITE exhibits a low hazard from accidental ingestion. However, it may

cause some irritation if splashed into the eyes. Should eye contact occur, flush with plenty of water. Splashes on the skin should be thoroughly washed with soap and water at the first opportunity. Contaminated clothing should be washed before reuse. When WHITE is used in the same equipment as BLUE, all of the WHITE should be removed before using BLUE. The two agents produce a white precipitate that will clog spray systems.

d. Soil Sterilants.

(1) *BROMACIL.*

(*a*) *Description.* BROMACIL is an odorless, noncorrosive, white crystalline solid, slightly soluble in water or diesel fuel oil. Three different forms are produced: HYVAR-X, a wettable powder containing 80-percent active ingredient; HYVAR-X-WS, a 50-percent active ingredient water-soluble powder; and UROX 'B', a liquid containing 4 pounds of active ingredient per gallon (app D).

(*b*) *Rate of application.* HYVAR-X is applied at a rate of 15 to 30 pounds per acre; HYVAR-X-WS, 24 to 48 pounds per acre; and UROX 'B', 3 to 6 gallons per acre. Spray concentrations of the agent as high as 50 to 150 pounds per 100 gallons of water or oil can be handled by aircraft-mounted spray systems. The 80-percent wettable powder is well suited for ground applications by power-driven decontaminating apparatus or turbine blower because it requires agitation while spraying to achieve the best results.

(2) *UROX 22.*

(*a*) *Description.* UROX 22 is a granular substance containing 22 percent monuron trichloroacetate.

(*b*) *Rate of application.* The manufacturer suggests using 150 to 200 pounds per acre.

(3) *Effect on foliage.* Soil sterilants act by absorption through the root system and therefore are most effective under conditions of good soil moisture. They are relatively stable once absorbed into the soil. Soil sterilants kill vegetation and may prevent regrowth for periods of a few months to a year, depending on the quantity and soil conditions. They are most

effective on grasses, but will control woody plants at higher application rates. Mechanical clearing by brush cutters or bulldozers is not necessary, but will help in getting the agent into the soil.

(4) *Safety precautions and handling.* Soil sterilants are only slightly corrosive to metals, but dispersion equipment should be thoroughly flushed after use. They are relatively nontoxic to humans, but respirator masks should be worn to prevent inhalation of dust during handling.

Section II
Concepts of Employment

53. General. *a.* The employment of antiplant agents must be carefully controlled by technically qualified personnel to avoid many undesirable aftereffects. FM 3-10 discusses the employment concepts, analysis of operations, and limitations of antiplant agents.

b. Guerrilla operations rely heavily on locally produced crops for their food supply. Crop destruction can reduce the food supply and seriously affect the guerrilla's survival. Naturally dense vegetation in jungle areas is ideal for elusive hit-and-run tactics of the guerrilla. Removal or reduction of this concealment limits the guerrilla's capability to operate in the defoliated area.

54. Employment Considerations. In addition to the concepts discussed in FM 3-10, the following points should be considered when planning the use of antiplant agents.

a. Type of Foliage. ORANGE is a wide-range, general-purpose agent which is effective on the many types of foliage found in jungle areas. WHITE is also considered a general-purpose herbicide, but it is generally slower than ORANGE. BLUE is most effective on the narrow leaf species: the grasses, sugarcane, rice, and other cereal grains.

b. When to Apply. The best time to apply antiplant agents is during the most active growing season. This corresponds roughly to the period from the appearance of new buds until 3 or 4 weeks before onset of the dry season. While spraying during the dry season does produce defoliation, vegetation is not killed as quickly as it is during the most active growing season. An exception would be in certain tropical lowland areas where water is plentiful and continuous growth exists; thus antiplant agents are effective throughout the year.

c. *Effect on Nearby Crops.* If the application of antiplant agents is on target to begin with, the main danger to nearby susceptible crops will be from drift. The main factors affecting agent drift are wind direction and speed, dissemination method (para 56 through 58), temperature gradient (TM 3-240), and the agent used. Conditions for dissemination of antiplant agents are usually most favorable during early morning hours (before 0800) while inversion temperature gradient prevails and the wind speed is still low (does not exceed 8 knots). A volatile antiplant agent may also produce drift effect even after the spray has settled on target. For example, the slight vaporization of ORANGE may produce drift damage, especially if nearby crops, such as rubber trees, cotton, melons, bananas, and other garden species, are *highly* susceptible to damage. Water-soluble agents BLUE and WHITE are not subject to vaporization after settling on target. Thus they can be more safely used near susceptible crops provided cautions such as wind direction are heeded, and a dissemination method that tends to produce the least amount of drift is used. Although soil sterilants do not drift, they should not be used closer than 100 meters to crops or cropland in a friendly area onto which drainage from treated areas flows.

d. *Duration of Effect.* Neither ORANGE, BLUE, nor WHITE can be considered "permanent" type antiplant agents. They act by direct contact with the plant. Defoliation resulting from aerial application of BLUE may be effective only until new growth appears. Defoliation resulting from aerial application of ORANGE or WHITE will usually be effective for one growing season, but may be effective for periods of approximately 9 months to 1 year. Soil sterilants, on the other hand, may be effective for periods of up to a year or more, because they are designed to be slowly dissolved by rainfall and remain active in the soil.

55. Symptoms of Plant Injury. The following symptoms of plant injury may be used to aid in evaluating the effectiveness of defoliation projects. Plants usually react to antiplant agents in one or more of these ways:

a. In some plants, leaves and growing stems form loops and coils or develop marked curvature.

b. Growing stems may remain green, but may swell, develop cracks, and form callous tissue.

c. Watery, translucent buds often appear at the crowns of some plants.

d. Spongy, enlarged roots may appear, turn black or gray, and rot.

e. Dead areas will form on the leaves wherever the spray droplets have settled on the leaf surface. A yellow ring may appear around the dead area, and gradually the entire leaf will develop yellow, brown, or red autumnal coloration and fall.

Section III
Dissemination Methods

56. General. Antiplant agents may be disseminated by various methods depending on the size of the area to be defoliated and whether the agent is in liquid, slurry, or solid form.

57. Ground-Based Application. Ground-based spray or dispersion methods are suited to small-scale operations such as defoliation around base camps or installations or clearing along routes of communication. These methods depend on easy access to the area on foot or by spray vechicle.

a. Hand broadcasting is the simplest way to disperse dry agents, such as soil sterilants, but is a rather time-consuming method.

b. A 3-gallon hand-pump sprayer is easy to use in areas accessible by foot but where vehicles cannot enter. It is a slow method, however, and areas out of arm's reach are still inaccessible.

c. The M106 Mity Mite (para 26) may be used to disperse liquid or dry antiplant agents. Foot access to the area is required, but inaccessible areas may be covered to some extent, since the Mity Mite will spray a distance of about 50 feet.

d. A power-driven decontaminating apparatus (PDDA) may be used when the area is accessible to wheeled vehicles. It is especially suited for spraying soil sterilant in slurry form. The PDDA may also be used to spray liquid antiplant agents. WHITE and BLUE present no corrosion problems, but the apparatus must be well cleaned when changing between the two agents. ORANGE will soften the rubber parts, such as hoses and valve diaphragms, requiring their replacement after a while. Spraying ORANGE by PDDA also produces a fire hazard.

e. Commercial orchard sprayers, if available, may be used for spraying liquid solutions where ground access to vehicles is possible.

58. Aerial Spray Methods. Aerial spray methods are suited for large-scale operations since a larger area can be covered and ground access is not necessary. Aerial application methods are much more subject to weather conditions, such as wind direction and speed and temperature gradient, than are ground-based methods. Therefore, particular attention must be paid to the possibility of agent drift onto any nearby friendly crops. The height of attack, airspeed, and area coverage depend on weather and terrain conditions and pilot experience.

a. UC-123 Aircraft. UC-123B cargo aircraft fitted with internal tanks and external spray booms are used for large-scale defoliation and crop destruction operations. Using the present systems at an altitude of 150 feet and airspeed of 130 knots results in a spray rate of 3 gallons per acre.

b. FIDAL (Fixed-wing Insecticide Disperal Apparatus, Liquid). The FIDAL is a Navy developed and tested system. It has not been standardized by the Army. When available, it can be used to supplement the spray capability of the C-123 systems. The FIDAL is hung on the AIE or A1H aircraft without modification. Each tank holds about 275 gallons and has its own ram turbine to provide power for pumping the spray through a spray boom. Cost is much less than that of C-123 inboard systems, and spray missions do not tie up the aircraft since the tanks can be hung or removed in minutes.

c. Helicopter-Mounted Spray Systems.

(1) *HIDAL* (*Helicopter Insecticide Dispersal Apparatus, Liquid*). The HIDAL system is a 196-gallon spray system suitable for use in a UH-1 series helicopter. Helicopters are useful in spraying areas around installations that are not accessible to wheeled vehicles: minefields, barbed wire barriers, etc. The HIDAL is self-contained, has an adjustable spray rate, and can be installed and removed in a matter of minutes. It is a Navy developed system and has not been standardized by the Army.

(2) *AGAVENCO sprayer.* The AGAVENCO system has capabilities similar to those of the HIDAL and is presently being procured in a limited quantity. It has not been standardized.

d. Field Expedient Spray Systems. When systems such as the HIDAL are unavailable, field expedient spray systems that will perform adequately might be constructed.

(1) *UH-1 series aircraft.*

(*a*) A simple expedient spray system for a UH-1 type aircraft might consist of a 55-gallon drum (fig 41 and 42) fitted with a rubber hose which delivers the solution to a spray bar temporarily mounted across the skids. Slight pressurization of the drum will usually help empty the drum at a steady rate. A portable flamethrower pressure bottle or an AN-M4 compressor can be used for pressurizing, but a gage should be in the system to warn of excess pressure (no more than 8 to 12 psi should be used). The size and number of holes in the spray bar may be determined by trial and error; however, ⅛-inch holes spaced 6 inches apart will provide good results.

(*b*) Another field expedient system uses the tank and 16-foot boom of the HIDAL. A 25-gpm personnel carrier bilge pump delivers the agent, allowing 30 to 40 meters coverage in width.

(2) *CH-47 aircraft.* An expedient spray system for a CH-47 aircraft might consist of a 500-gallon collapsible fuel bladder or a 400-gallon metal, skid-mounted tank. A power driven fuel transfer pump (50 to 100 gpm) can be used to deliver the antiplant agent to a spray bar attached to the ramp at the rear of the aircraft.

ANTIPLANT AGENT USE RATES[1]

Vegetation type	Orange	White	Blue[2]
Mangrove	1½ gal/acre	3-5 gal/acre	2 gal/acre
Highland trees (jungle)	3 gal/acre	3-5 gal/acre	2 gal/acre
Mixed mangrove, low land swamp, scrub trees	3 gal/acre	3-5 gal/acre	2 gal/acre
Broadleaf crops (bean, manioc, corn, banana, tomato)	1 gal/acre	3-5 gal/acre	2 gal/acre
Rice	5 gal/acre	3-5 gal/acre	1 gal/acre
Mixed vegetables and rice	3 gal/acre	3-5 gal/acre	2 gal/acre

[1] As recommended by the manufacturer.
[2] Usually applied in the field by C123 aircraft systems having fixed flow of 3 gal/acre.

COMPOSITION OF MILITARILY SIGNIFICANT
ANTIPLANT AGENTS

Antiplant agent	Composition
ORANGE	50% 2,4-D (n-butyl-2,4-dichlorophenoxyace-tate) 50% 2,4,5-T (n-butyl-2,4,5-trichlorophenoxy-acetate)
WHITE	20% picloram (4-amino-3,5,6-trichloropico-linic acid) 80% 2,4-D (triisopropanolamine)
BLUE (Phytar 560G)	3 pounds per gallon of water of: 65% cacodylic acid (dimethylarsenic acid) 35% inert ingredients: sodium chloride, sodium and calcium sulfates, water
BROMACIL	Active ingredient: 5-bromo-3-sec-butyl-6-methyluracil HYVAR-X: 80% active ingredient HYVAR-X-WS: 50% active ingredient UROX 'B'—liquid, 4 pounds per gallon active ingredient
UROX 22	22% monuron trichloroacetate, 78% inert in-gredients

AREA TREATED WITH HERBICIDES IN SOUTH VIETNAM 1962–1969

Year	Defoliation	Crop Destruction
1962	4,940 *acres*	741 *acres*
1963	24,700	247
1964	83,486	10,374
1965	155,610	65,949
1966	741,247	101,517
1967	1,486,446	221,312
1968	1,267,110	63,726
1969 (*Jan-Mar*)	356,421	4,693
	4,119,960	468,559

Source: Military Assistance Command Vietnam Reports

STATEMENT BY
REAR ADMIRAL WILLIAM E. LEMOS
POLICY PLANS AND
NATIONAL SECURITY COUNCIL
AFFAIRS OFFICE,
ASSISTANT SECRETARY
(INTERNATIONAL SECURITY AFFAIRS)
DEPARTMENT OF DEFENSE

*Delivered before the Subcommittee on
National Security Policy and Scientific
Developments
Committee on Foreign Affairs
House of Representatives
First Session, 91st Congress
on Herbicide Operations*

Turning now to the use of herbicides in Vietnam, one of the most difficult problems of military operations in South Vietnam is the inability to observe the enemy in the dense forest and jungle. Defoliating herbicides introduced in 1962 are capable of producing a significant improvement in vertical and horizontal visibility in the type of jungle found in South Vietnam. As viewed by an aerial observer, it is often impossible to see through the canopy to detect VC or NVA operations. In 6 to 8 weeks, after spraying with a herbicide, the observer will have good observation through the canopy. For ground observation, defoliation is highly effective in improving horizontal visibility.

The Herbicide Program in terms of effects produced has required an unusually small investment of military effort. The entire program has been accomplished with an average of about

17 C-123 spray aircraft and several smaller helicopter sprayers plus some improvised ground spray equipment.

Herbicide operations are conducted under a program directed by the Government of South Vietnam. Requests for these operations generally originate at the district or provincial level and are submitted through territorial administration command channels. The herbicide spray plan includes as a minimum the area requested to be treated with herbicide, the public information, civil affairs and intelligence annexes, along with a statement by the province chief that he will see that just and legal claims are paid for any accidental damage. The ARVN corps commanders and their US corps senior advisors have been delegated authority to approve small scale defoliation by ground-based spray and by helicopters. All requests for crop destruction and larger scale defoliation by C-123 aircraft are forwarded to the Vietnamese Joint General Staff. Upon approval of the request by the Chief of Joint General Staff it is forwarded to the MACV staff for final review.

The MACV staff position is developed as the result of coordination with CORDS (Civil Operations and Revolutionary Development Support), USAID, and political representatives at each level where they exist. An aerial reconnaissance is conducted as the next step to ensure that all populated areas and friendly crops have been excluded from the target area. Having determined from this aerial survey and an analysis of the military worth that the project is a valid herbicide target, the project is forwarded to the US Ambassador and COMUSMACV for approval. The Ambassador personally approves all C-123 defoliation projects and all enemy crop destruction projects.

Some specific uses of herbicides are:

1. *Defoliation of Base Perimeters.*

A portion of the small scale ground based or the helicopter spray missions are used in improving the defense of base camps and fire bases. Herbicides are a great help in keeping down the growth of high jungle grass, bushes and weeds which will grow in cleared areas near these camps. This clearance opens fields of fire and affords observation for outposts to prevent surprise attack and as such is truly a life-saving measure for our forces and our allies. Without the use of herbicides around our fire bases, adequate defense is difficult and in many places impossible.

2. *Defoliation of Lines of Communication.*

There are many instances of ambush sites being defoliated for better aerial observation and improved visibility along roads and trails. In 1967 there were also many requests for defoliation of VC tax collection points. In otherwise friendly territory there were points along well travelled routes where the enemy could hide under cover and intercept travellers to demand taxes. Defoliation along these roads was very effective in opening these areas so that they can be seen from observation aircraft, and with few exceptions these roads were opened to free travel. The use of aircraft to spray alongside lines of communication proved valuable in clearing these areas and preventing costly ambush of army convoys with resulting friendly casualties.

3. *Defoliation of Infiltration Routes.*

Areas used by the enemy for routes of approach, resupply or movement are targets for herbicide spray. Probably the most valuable use of herbicides for defoliation is to permit aerial observation in such areas. This is particularly true in areas near the border so that we can detect movement of enemy units and their resupply.

4. *Defoliation of Enemy Base Camps.*

We know from prisoners of war and from observation that the enemy will move from areas that have been sprayed. Therefore, enemy base camps or unit headquarters are sprayed in order to make him move to avoid exposing himself to aerial observation. If he does move back in while the area is still defoliated, he will be observed and can be engaged.

5. *Crop Destruction.*

Crops in areas remote from the friendly population and known to belong to the enemy and which cannot be captured by ground operations are sometimes sprayed. Such targets are carefully selected so as to attack only those crops known to be grown by or for the VC or NVA. The authorization to attack crops in specific areas has been made by the US Embassy, Saigon, MACV and South Vietnamese Government.

Frequent reviews have been conducted of the Herbicide Program. The most recent one was personally directed and reviewed by COMUSMACV in October 1968 to assure himself that the program was militarily effective. Prior to that, the US Ambassador had directed a review which looked at the political and economic aspects of the program. The Embassy report was released in August 1968. The crop destruction program was also reviewed by the CINCPAC Scientific Advisor in December 1967. Each of these reports concluded that the program should be continued.

The requests for defoliation and crop destruction have always exceeded our capability to spray. The requirement continues although a tapering off should develop if enemy activity subsides. A recent review by MACV indicated that operations for 1970 will be less than in 1969. In addition, Rome plows are replacing defoliation for clearing along many lines of communication.

With regard to the recent publicity of the herbicide agent, 2,4,5-T, which is a component of Orange, a herbicide mixture, the Bionetics Research Laboratories conducted a study of the carcinogenic, teratogenic and mutagenic activity of selected pesticides and industrial chemicals for the National Cancer Institute during the period 1965-1968. The study indicated that a large dose of 2,4,5-T administered orally to specific strains of mice during the central portion of the gestation period produced abnormal fetuses.

However, on 29 October 1969, Dr. DuBridge, Science Advisor to the President, stated, "It seems improbable that any person could receive harmful amounts of this chemical from any of the existing uses of 2,4,5-T."

Nevertheless, Deputy Secretary of Defense David Packard has issued instructions to the Joint Chiefs of Staff to reemphasize the already existing policy that 2,4,5-T be utilized only in areas remote from population.

When the American Embassy conducted the political and

economic review of the herbicide program, it requested that a disinterested expert be sent from the United States to assess any ecological consequences of the program. Dr. Fred Tschirley, Agricultural Research Service, Department of Agriculture, was sent over in March 1968 for a one-month period. Arrangements were made which permitted him to fly over any area of Vietnam he wished to inspect plus on-the-ground visits to any safe area. He concluded that the defoliation program had caused some ecological changes. Although single treatment on semideciduous forest would cause inconsequential changes, repeated treatments could kill enough trees to permit invasion of many sites by bamboo. The presence of bamboo would then retard regeneration of the forest.

The Army supports the need for a more detailed investigation of the ecological effects of herbicides used in Vietnam. Such an investigation should be conducted in coordination with other interested agencies. In order to get such a study started, a research and development project entitled "Ecological Effects of the Military Use of Herbicides in Vietnam" is being initiated. This study would continue into the post-hostilities phase.

In the final analysis the sole purpose of the herbicide program is to protect friendly forces and conserve manpower. The following examples should demonstrate the success of the defoliation effort in Vietnam:

1. Major defoliation has been accomplished in War Zone C. Prior to defoliation, 7 brigades were necessary to maintain US/GVN presence. During 1967, after defoliation only 3 brigades were required.

2. The Commander of Naval Forces in Vietnam in a report to General Abrams stated: "As you know, a major concern is the vegetation along the main shipping channel. Your continuing efforts under difficult and hazardous flying conditions, in keeping this area and the adjacent inland areas devoid of vegetation have contributed considerably in denying the protective cover from which to ambush the slow-moving merchant ships and US Navy craft."

3. In 1968, the Commanding General of the First Field

Force reported: "Defoliation has been effective in enhancing the success of allied combat operations. Herbicide operations using C-123 aircraft, helicopters, truck mounted and hand sprayers have become an integral part of the II CTZ operations against VC/NVA. The operations are normally limited to areas under VC/NVA control remote from population centers. The defoliation program has resulted in the reduction of enemy concealment and permitted increased use of supply routes by friendly units. Aerial surveillance of enemy areas has improved and less security forces are required to control areas of responsibility. An overall result of the herbicide program has been to increase friendly security and to assist in returning civilians to GVN control."

4. The US Commander in the III CTZ related: "Herbicide operations have contributed significantly to allied combat operations in the III Corps. Defoliation is an important adjunct to target acquisition. Aerial photographs can often be taken from which interpreters can 'see the ground' in areas that previously were obscured. Defoliation also aids visual reconnaissance. USAF FAC's (forward air controllers) and US Army aerial observers have discovered entire VC base camps in defoliated areas that had previously been overlooked."

5. In the south in the IV CTZ, C-123 herbicide operations are limited. This is because of the vast areas of valuable crops which are not to be destroyed, even though they may be in enemy hands. Therefore, the commander of the IV Corps area in presenting his evaluation cited the value of helicopter operations as follows: "A significant helicopter defoliation mission was conducted in the vicinity of SADEC in August 1968. The target area consisted of 3 main canals which converged and formed a strong VC base. The dense vegetation permitted visibility of only 10-15 meters horizontally and nil vertically. The area was sprayed with approximately 735 gallons of herbicide White and over 90 percent of the area was defoliated. As a result of the defoliation, an ARVN battalion was able to remain overnight in the area for the first time in five years. Many enemy bunkers were open to observation. Since the defoliation,

the VC presence has decreased to the point that only RF/PF forces are now necessary for local security."

6. As a part of the 1968 evaluation report of herbicide operations, the US Senior Advisor in the IV Corps Tactical Zone area reported: "A section of National Highway 4 in Phong Dinh Province was the site for a defoliation operation on 24 June 1968. Since January 1968, a series of ambushes was conducted against SVN convoys and troop movements. Because of the total inability of ground troops to keep the area clear of VC, this area was sprayed using 685 gallons of herbicide White. The target area was primarily coconut palm and banana trees that had been abandoned by their owners for several years. During the period of abandonment the vegetation had become so dense that convoy security elements were not able to see more than five meters into the underbrush and had to rely on reconnaissance by fire to discover the hidden enemy. This method of protection had proven ineffective. Three RF/PF companies with US advisors were used to secure the target for the helicopter operation in addition to an armored cavalry troop. Since the defoliation mission was completed, convoys have used the highway 2 or 3 times a week without attack or harassment. Only one RF platoon has remained in the area to provide local security to the hamlet and highway."

7. In certain instances, we know the VC have been forced to divert tactical units from combat missions to food-procurement operations and food-transportation tasks, attesting to the effectiveness of the crop destruction program. In local areas where extensive crop destruction missions were conducted, VC/NVA defections to GVN increased as a result of low morale resulting principally from food shortages.

The most highly valued item of equipment to field commanders in Vietnam is the helicopter. There was some question when the helicopter spray equipment was first procured whether field commanders would divert the use of helicopters from combat operations for herbicide spray operations. The very fact that the commanders have used their helicopter spray equipment to the fullest and have asked for more is certainly proof that herbicide operations have been helpful in protecting the American soldier and contributing to successful accomplishment of the ground combat mission.

DUBRIDGE STATEMENT

Executive Office of the President
Office of Science and Technology

October 29, 1969

Dr. Lee A. DuBridge, Science Adviser to the President and Executive Secretary of the President's Environmental Quality Council, announced today a coordinated series of actions that that are being taken by the agencies of Government to restrict the use of the weed-killing chemical, 2,4,5-T.

The actions to control the use of the chemical were taken as a result of findings from a laboratory study conducted by Bionetics Research Laboratories which indicated that offspring of mice and rats given relatively large oral doses of the herbicide during early stages of pregnancy showed a higher than expected number of deformities.

Although it seems improbable that any person could receive harmful amounts of this chemical from any of the existing uses of 2,4,5-T, and while the relationships of these effects in laboratory animals to effects in man are not entirely clear at this time, the actions taken will assure safety of the public while further evidence is being sought.

The study involved relatively small numbers of laboratory rats and mice. More extensive studies are needed and will be undertaken. At best it is difficult to extrapolate results obtained with laboratory animals to man—sensitivity to a given compound may be different in man than in animal species; metabolic pathways may be different.

2,4,5-T is highly effective in control of many species of broadleaf weeds and woody plants, and is used on ditch banks, along roadsides, on rangelands, and other places. Almost none is used by home gardeners or in residential areas. The chemical is effective in defoliating trees and shrubs and its use in South Vietnam has resulted in reducing greatly the number of ambushes, thus saving lives. The following actions are being taken:

The Department of Agriculture will cancel registrations of 2,4,5-T for use on food crops effective January 1, 1970, unless by that time the Food and Drug Administration has found a basis for establishing a safe legal tolerance in and on foods.

The Department of Health, Education, and Welfare will complete action on the petition requesting a finite tolerance for 2,4,5-T residues on foods prior to January 1, 1970.

The Departments of Agriculture and Interior will stop use in their own programs of 2,4,5-T in populated areas or where residues from use could otherwise reach man.

The Department of Defense will restrict the use of 2,4,5-T to areas remote from the population.

Other Departments of the Government will take such actions in their own programs as may be consistent with these announced plans.

The Department of State will advise other countries of the actions being taken by the United States to protect the health of its citizens and will make available to such countries the technical data on which these decisions rest.

Appropriate Departments of Government will undertake immediately to verify and extend the available experimental evidence so as to provide the best technical basis possible for such future actions as the Government might wish to undertake with respect to 2,4,5-T and similar compounds.

STATEMENT BY THE PRESIDENT ON BIOLOGICAL DEFENSE POLICIES AND PROGRAMS

The White House

November 25, 1969

Soon after taking office I directed a comprehensive study of our chemical and biological defense policies and programs. There had been no such review in over fifteen years. As a result, objectives and policies in this field were unclear and programs lacked definition and direction.

Under the auspices of the National Security Council, the Departments of State and Defense, the Arms Control and Disarmament Agency, the Office of Science and Technology, the Intelligence Community and other agenices worked closely together on this study for over six months. These government efforts were aided by contributions from the scientific community through the President's Scientific Advisory Committee.

This study has now been completed and its findings carefully considered by the National Secuity Council. I am now reporting the decisions taken on the basis of this review.

Chemical Warfare Program

As to our chemical warfare program, the United States:

Reaffirms its oft-repeated renunciation of the first use of lethal chemical weapons.

Extends this renunciation to the first use of incapacitating chemicals.

Consonant with these decisions, the Administration will submit to the Senate, for its advice and consent to ratification, The Geneva Protocol of 1925 which prohibits the first use in war of "asphyxiating, poisonous or other Gases and of Bacteriological Methods of Warfare." The United States has long supported the principles and objectives of this Protocol. We take this step toward formal ratification to reinforce our continuing advocacy of international constraints on the use of these weapons.

Biological Research Program

Biological weapons have massive, unpredictable and potentially uncontrollable consequences. They may produce global epidemics and impair the health of future generations. I have therefore decided that:

The U.S. shall renounce the use of lethal biological agents and weapons, and all other methods of biological warfare.

The U.S. will confine its biological research to defensive measures such as immunization and safety measures.

The DOD has been asked to make recommendations as to the disposal of existing stocks of bacteriological weapons.

In the spirit of these decisions, the United States associates itself with the principles and objectives of the United Kingdom Draft Convention which would ban the use of Biological methods of warfare. We will seek, however, to clarify specific provisions of the draft to assure that necessary safeguards are included.

Neither our association with the Convention nor the limiting of our program to research will leave us vulnerable to surprise by an enemy who does not observe these rational restraints. Our intelligence community will continue to watch carefully the nature and extent of the biological programs of others.

These important decisions, which have been announced today, have been taken as an initiative toward peace. Mankind already carries in its own hands too many of the seeds of its own destruction. By the examples we set today, we hope to contribute to an atmosphere of peace and understanding between nations and among men.

RESOLUTION PASSED BY THE COUNCIL OF THE AMERICAN ASSOCIATION FOR THE ADVANCEMENT OF SCIENCE

December 30, 1969
Boston, Massachusetts

Whereas, recent studies commissioned by the National Cancer Institute have shown that 2,4,5-T and 2,4-D cause birth malformations in experimental animals, and

Whereas, the above studies conclude that 2,4,5-T is probably dangerous to man, and that 2,4-D is potentially dangerous to man, and

Whereas, 2,4,5-T and 2,4-D are widely used for military defoliation in Vietnam in amounts (20 to 30 lbs/acre) that are much greater than those used in civilian operations, and

Whereas, there is a possibility that the use of herbicides in Vietnam is causing birth malformations among infants of exposed mothers;

Therefore, be it resolved that the Council of AAAS urge that the U.S. Department of Defense immediately cease all use of 2,4-D and 2,4,5-T in Vietnam.

STATEMENT
OF DR. ARTHUR W. GALSTON,
PROFESSOR OF BIOLOGY AND
LECTURER IN FORESTRY,
YALE UNIVERSITY

Delivered before the Subcommittee on
National Security Policy and Scientific
Developments of the Committee on Foreign
Affairs House of Representatives

December, 1969

Use of Herbicides as Weapons

MR. GALSTON. I am a botanist, and I would like to confine my remarks to the use of herbicides as military weapons in Vietnam, with some overtones concerning the social and health implications of their use in the United States.

Since 1962, about 4 million acres of Vietnam have been sprayed with about 100 million pounds of assorted herbicides. This is an area about the size of the State of Massachusetts.

The agents which have been used in Vietnam may be classed into three types of chemicals: The first type, Agent Orange, consists of two commonly used phenoxyacetic acids that go by the shorthand names of 2,4-D and 2,4,5-T.

They are used in Vietnam at about 27 pounds per acre, and I should say parenthetically that this is up to 10 times the usual domestic dose recommended.

Agent White is a mixture of 2,4-D and a fairly new chemical

called picloram or tordon. This mixture is sprayed so as to deposit about 6 pounds of 2,4-D and 1½ pounds of picloram per acre.

The third agent, called Agent Blue, is known chemically as cacodylic acid. It is an arsenic-containing material, and is sprayed at the rate of about 9.3 pounds per acre.

As Mr. Swyter has already mentioned, the main object of our use of these chemicals is to defoliate around trails, estuaries and encampments to prevent ambush, infiltration and military buildups. By all odds, this use of these chemicals appears to have been militarily successful.

A secondary use has to do mainly with cacodylic acid, a chemical uniquely adapted to kill grass plants such as rice. We spray and kill rice in paddies of outlying areas which are suspected of being supply centers for bands of guerrillas. In some instances entire villages are suspected of being Vietcong sympathizers; killing their food crops prevents their use as a staging area for any sort of military operations and has in some instances led to complete abandonment of the village.

All of these chemicals are in use in the United States. Their use was initiated on a large scale at about the end of World War II. In fact, 2,4-D and its relative 2,4,5-T were developed in what is now known as Fort Detrick. The early formulations were made there, and the use of these chemicals as agriculturally important herbicides and plant growth regulators stemmed in part from those early military investigations.

It has been assumed, because of the rapid breakdown of 2,4-D in the soil, that the massive use of this chemical does not constitute a health hazard. I shall have occasion to return to this point, because recent evidence indicates that not only 2,4-D, but more importantly, its relative 2,4,5-T, may constitute an important health hazard, both at home and in Vietnam.

Underscore Effects of Herbicide Use

The kinds of undesirable consequences that flow from our massive use of herbicides can be summarized under three general headings. Some of these have been already alluded to briefly by Mr. Swyter, and I hope I may enlarge on them.

One is ecological damage; the second would be inadvertent agricultural damage, and the third involves direct damage to people.

1. *Ecological Damage*   Under ecological damage, it has already been well documented that some kinds of plant associations subject to spray, especially by Agent Orange, containing 2,4-D and 2,4,5-T, have been irreversibly damaged. I refer specifically to the mangrove associations that line the estuaries, especially around the Saigon River.

Up to 100,000 acres of these mangroves have been sprayed. In a report published in *Science* about a year ago,[1] Dr. Fred Tschirley, who went to Vietnam at the behest of the U.S. State Department, confirmed that there was extensive killing of these mangrove associations by one spray of 2,4-D. Some of them had been sprayed as early as 1961 and have shown no substantial signs of recovery. Ecologists have estimated a minimum of 20-25 years for effective recovery to occur.

You might ask why we should be concerned with the mangrove associations. What are they to us? Ecologists have known for a long time that the mangroves lining estuaries furnish one of the most important ecological niches for the completion of the life cycle of certain shellfish and migratory fish. If these plant communities are not in a healthy state, secondary effects on the whole interlocked web of organisms are bound to occur.

So not only is there now likely to be increased erosion along the estuaries, and destruction of that stable environment, but in the years ahead the Vietnamese, who do not have overabundant sources of proteins anyhow, are probably going to suffer dietarily because of the deprivation of food in the form of fish and shellfish. I would assume that the United States will have to assume the major responsibility for making up the deficiency.

---

[1] Tschirley, F. H., "Defoliation in Vietnam," Science 163: 779–786, 1969.

Damage to Soil

Damage to the soil is another possible consequence of extensive defoliation. It has been minimized by some, but I think we
will find, when we look at Vietnam in detail after hostilities are
over, that there has been considerable damage done to the soil
in various parts of the country. I state this firmly, as a conviction
which I have as a botanist.

We know that the soil is not a dead, inert mass, but, rather,
that it is a vibrant, living community. Up to one-half of the
total weight of some soils can be micro-organisms who derive
their food from the organic matter excreted from the fine roots
of trees and other vegetation growing in any area. If you knock
the leaves off of trees once, twice or three times, whether you
kill them or not, you interfere with the excretion of organic
matter into the soil; you cause an alteration in the level of
activity of these microbes; you change the quality of the soil.

We know from our own soils that microbes are important in
that they synthesize gummy substances which cement the soil
particles together. This gives us the crumb structure that the
agriculturalist knows is essential for good tilth, with good
aeration, good water- and mineral-holding capacity and good
quality for the growth of roots. Failing the microbial activity,
we could have compaction of soil particles into hard clays, into
which roots have difficulty penetrating. If this occurs agricultural productivity declines markedly, and recovery may be a
very slow process.

Worse than this, certain tropical soils—and it has been
estimated that in Vietnam up to 50 percent of all the soils fall
into this category—are laterizable; that is, they may be irreversibly converted to rock as a result of their deprivation of
organic matter. Many tropical soils are very weak in what the
agriculturalist knows as base exchange capacity. The only thing
that stabilizes the soil is its organic matter. If, as I have mentioned earlier, you deprive trees of their leaves and photosyn-

thesis stops, organic matter in the soil declines and laterization, the making of brick, may occur on a very extensive scale. I would emphasize that this brick is irreversibly hardened; it cannot be made back into soil, short of breaking it up with a sledge hammer or similar device. Part of the Temple of Angkor Wat in Cambodia is made of laterized soil. The fact that this temple has been around for 11 centuries is a testimonial to the persistence of such material.

Another ecological consequence is the invasion of an area by undesirable plants. One of the main plants that invades an area that has been defoliated is bamboo. Bamboo is one of the most difficult of all plants to destroy once it becomes established where you don't want it. It is not amenable to killing by herbicides. Frequently it has to be burned over, and this causes tremendous dislocations to agriculture.

Dangers of Picloram

Finally, in the line of ecological damage, I would note that the recently introduced chemical picloram is one of the longest lived pesticides I know of in soil. I believe it to be a herbicidal analog of DDT. As we all know, DDT, introduced into our ecosystem, persists for years and years. Picloram is not quite that long lived, but it is very long lived, indeed, compared with any other herbicide.

In "Down to Earth," a publication of the Dow Chemical Co., which synthesizes this material, I have read that less than 3½ percent of the applied picloram disappeared from certain California clay soils in a field trial lasting 467 days. In other soils, the disappearance is up to 20 percent of the applied material in 467 days.

It is clear that picloram, once applied, could be around for years. I would suggest that its massive application to the soils of Vietnam is going to hamper agriculture, even after hostilities are over, for some time into the future.

2. *Inadvertent Agricultural Damage* My second category of damage is inadvertent agricultural damage. There are many useful plants growing in all parts of South Vietnam. When one flies over a forested area that one wishes to defoliate, with a converted cargo plane carrying tanks of herbicidal liquid delivered through high-pressure nozzles, one hopes that one has gaged the meteorological situation accurately and that the fine droplets produced by these nozzles will, in fact, fall on areas whose spraying is desired.

It is understandable, weather being what it is, that winds come up occasionally, that meteorological patterns change drastically, and that pilots miss the mark. All sorts of inadvertent accident can happen. Finishing a run with some gallons left in the tank, and jettisoning the rest, may cause it to fall in areas not desired, as the Skull Valley accident made dramatically clear.

We have documentation of several very important accidents of this kind in Vietnam. For example, thousands of trees in the Michelin rubber plantation to the north and west of Saigon were injured a few years ago following a spray operation. Some trees were killed, some recovered slowly, but the United States has compensated the French owners of that rubber plantation at the rate of $87 per tree.

In Cambodia, we are now facing a lawsuit by the Cambodian Government to the extent of about $9 million, resulting from extensive spraying in the Tay Ninh Province of neighboring South Vietnam. The report of the investigation team, which included Dr. Fred H. Tschirley and Dr. Charles Minarik of Fort Detrick, concluded that only a part of the damage is due to inadvertent drift. Some damage appears to have been due to deliberate spraying over the Cambodian border. In any event some 700 square kilometers of territory were affected, and the outcome of this lawsuit is still to be determined.

There have been documented reports of extensive damage to truck crops grown along roads, trails, and canals near Saigon. This results, I believe, from the drifting of herbicide from regions where they were intended to be deposited, over to areas in which truck farms were being cultivated. I believe the extent of this damage has not been accurately calculated, but certainly must go into the millions of dollars.

3. Damage to People Finally, I would like to discuss the most recent danger of the use of these herbicides to come to light. I refer to their direct damage to people. It is a source of great distress to me to find that some 25 years after the first introduction of the chlorinated phenoxyacetic acids like 2,4-D and 2,4,5-T, which together constitute about a $40 million business in this country today, that there have not been published before this year adequate toxicological data to support their extensive use in agriculture.

We have depended upon the fact that 2,4-D is rapidly degraded in soil by micro-organisms. We usually say its half-life is just a few weeks. 2,4,5-T, with just one extra chlorine atom on the benzene ring, is substantially longer lived. It is this chemical which has now been shown to be harmful to animals, although 2,4-D is also suspect.

About 2 years ago, a toxicological study was commissioned by the National Institutes of Health, and carried out by a private research organization called the Bionetics Research Laboratory in Bethesda, Md.

Three kinds of tests were made on a large number of commonly used agricultural chemicals. One involved mutagenicity; that is, do the chemicals cause mutations? This test was carried out against micro-organisms. Second, are the chemicals carcinogenic? Do they produce cancers when injected into test organisms such as mice? Thirdly, are they teratogenic; that is, do they cause malformations in developing embryos?

Teratogenic Effects of 2,4,5-T

The teratogenic chemical with which most of us are familiar is, of course, thalidomide. It has recently been divulged that

2,4,5-T is one of the most teratogenic chemicals known. In experiments by the Bionetics Laboratory in which 2,4,5-T was fed in the diet, in honey, from 4.6 up to 113 milligrams per kilogram of body weight, extensive teratogenic damage was noted. Even at the lowest dose I have quoted, 4.6 milligrams per kilogram, there was marked enlargement of the liver of the mother. This shows that the body was trying to cope with this extra burden, trying to detoxify the chemical which was applied. This dose also produced a significant rise in abnormal births in rats.

If the chemical was injected subcutaneously, the damage was somewhat greater. At the highest concentration used, 113 milligrams per kilogram body weight, which is equivalent to only a [fraction of an ounce], for a human, 100 percent of all of the litters born had at least one abnormality, and up to 70 percent of all the offspring were abnormal in some major respect.

The abnormalities include lack of heads, lack of eyes, faulty eyes, cystic kidneys, cleft palate, enlarged livers, and other types of damage which toxicologists and teratologists feel are very significant.

The results with mice were so striking that tests were conducted with rats, and the rat tests confirmed the teratogenicity. I suppose the next step will be to test this chemical in rabbits, dogs, and then in primates.

When the President's science adviser, Dr. DuBridge, was made aware of these results, he issued an order which restrained the use of 2,4,5-T, both domestically and in Vietnam. As I understand it, as of the 1st of January 1970, 2,4,5-T, which is used massively domestically will not be available for agricultural usage, and its use will be restricted to clearing the underbrush from around powerlines, railway embankments, and the like. In Vietnam, its use in populated areas is to be discontinued. The Department of Defense has announced that this is consistent with present use, and that operations involving 2,4,5-T will proceed as before.

I suggest that its teratogenicity is such that even its use in such apparently innocuous domestic matters as clearing brush near powerlines is undesirable. Such chemicals could find their ways into water supplies, and could be ingested in teratogenic doses.

Effects of 2,4,5-T in Vietnam

We have sprayed 2,4,5-T exhaustively in Vietnam. Have we caused any damage to people there? One can't know for sure. All that one can do is put together various bits of evidence. We know that 27 pounds per acre are sprayed. Let us assume that 2,4-D is completely nontoxic, although the Bionetics report indicates that it, too, is suspect, and should be further investigated.

If you consider only the 2,4,5-T sprayed and assume that a 1-inch rainfall, which is quite common in South Vietnam, has occurred after the spray, then you can calculate that there are about 50 milligrams per liter of 2,4,5-T in the water. Most of the drinking water and cooking water in South Vietnam is gathered in two ways—either from very shallow wells, or from catching the rainwater from the rooftops and keeping it in cisterns.

If one assumes that a pregnant woman drinks a liter of water a day, which is certainly conservative, then she consumes about 1½ milligrams per kilo of body weight per day. While this is a little bit below the lowest level tested in the Bionetics survey, I would recall to you that even those lowest levels indicated some damage in the form of oversized livers and abnormal births. Furthermore we cannot be sure that humans are not more sensitive to the 2,4,5-T than are these test animals.

I would also like to suggest that if the rainfall were less or water consumption more or if there were uneven deposits of 2,4,5-T, then significant teratogenic events could have occurred among Vietnamese women.

Reports of Abnormal Births from Saigon

Is there any evidence that such damage has occurred? If one looks at the Saigon newspapers, one finds that since late 1967, which would coincide with the end of the first year of our massive spray operations, there have been numerous reports, in the Saigon newspapers, of the incidence, especially in two hospitals in Saigon, of a completely new kind of birth abnormality. It is called the "egg bundle-like fetus," pictures of which have been published on the front pages of some of the Saigon newspapers.

We do not know, of course, what is causing these abnormal births. There are many traumatic events occurring in South Vietnam, and we cannot say that 2,4,5-T is the trauma which is giving rise to these abnormal births. But I would say that the entire spectrum of events compels me, as a biologist, to examine current restrictions on the use of all of these chemicals, none of which has been tested adequately for effects on humans and animals close to humans. I would hope that further restrictions would be placed on the use of these chemicals until we are sure that they are not causing adverse effects on people at home as well as in Vietnam.

Like Mr. Swyter, I would hope that the herbicides would be included in those "asphyxiating, poisonous, and other gases and analogous liquids, materials, and devices" whose use is banned in the Geneva Protocol, which will shortly be resubmitted to the Senate for ratification.

I would hope that the Senate, and all others concerned with this problem would do all they can, in the light of the evidence which I have presented, to include herbicides in the ban.

REPORT ON HERBICIDAL DAMAGE
BY THE UNITED STATES
IN SOUTHEASTERN CAMBODIA

By A. H. Westing, E. W. Pfeiffer, J. Lavorel,
& L. Matarasso

Phnom Penh
December 31, 1969

Introduction

This is a preliminary report of a study of herbicidal damage by the United States in southeastern Cambodia carried out by an *ad hoc* international scientific commission. It is based upon four days of intensive field investigation during the period of 25 to 29 December 1969 and upon additional detailed interviews in Phnom Penh with M. Chuon Saodi, the Cambodian Minister of Agriculture, M. Min Sarim, the Director General of State Rubber Plantations, M. Suon Kaset, the Director of Waters, Forests, and Game, M. Hing Un, Director of Agriculture, M. Sor Thay Seng, Chief of the Division of Agronomy, and with other government officials.

Our study was made possible by the Royal Government of Cambodia, which supplied us with all land and air transportation and other help necessary to visit the areas in question and to otherwise perform our mission. Any and all areas we wished to visit were freely open to us for purposes of inspection, interviewing, and photography.

In the field we were at all time accompanied by one or more scientists and occasionally other officials of the Cambodian government (and by an armed guard while working along the

Vietnamese border). We received full cooperation and gracious hospitality wherever we went from the people at all levels of responsibility and in all walks of life. There was virtually no language barrier since French (and often English) was understood almost everywhere and since a Cambodian (Khmer) interpreter was always available to us as needed for communication with uneducated local inhabitants. M. Min Sarim, Director General of State Rubber Plantations (and a professional forester), accompanied us virtually at all times. He was most useful to us because of his close familiarity with most of the areas we visited and because of his knowledge of rubber culture, of forestry, and of agronomy. M. Min had studied for five years at the University of Quebec; he speaks Cambodian, French, and English.

It was our mission to make an independent scientific evaluation of the herbicidal damage done by the United States in April and May of 1969. One of our aims was to verify the earlier Cambodian and United States assessments of damage. We wished particularly to assess rate of recovery, extent of long-term effects, and the impact on the local inhabitants and their economy. A more general aim was to gain some preliminary insights into the ecological and economic damages caused by herbicidal chemical warfare in the light of its massive use by the United States in neighboring South Vietnam.

Personnel

The present study was conducted by a four-man *ad hoc* scientific commission, two members from France and two members from the United States:

1. JEAN LAVOREL (plant biophysicist)
Directeur de Recherche et Directeur du Laboratoire de Photosynthèse du Centre National de la Recherche Scientifique (CNRS)
91, Gif-Sur-Yvette, France

2. Léon Matarasso (lawyer)
Avocat à la Cour de Paris
Vice-Président du Centre International pour la Dénunciation
des Crimes de Guerre
29, Rue de Tournon, Paris, 6e, France
3. Egbert W. Pfeiffer (Ph.D.; animal physiologist)
Professor of Zoology, University of Montana, Missoula,
Montana 59801, U.S.A.
4. Arthur H. Westing (M.F., Ph.D.; plant physiologist)
Associate Professor of Botany & Chairman of Biology,
Windham College
Putney, Vermont 05346, U.S.A.

Field Itinerary

Thursday, 25 December 1969. Aerial examination by small reconnaissance plane of both damaged and undamaged rubber plantations and other lands. This was primarily over the undamaged Chup area and over the damaged areas of Krek, Chalang (Chalong), Mimot, (Mémot) and vicinity—all in the southeastern border province of Kompong Cham (adjacent to the South Vietnamese province of Tay Ninh).

Friday, 26 December 1969. Visit to the Cambodian Rubber Research Institute (Institut des Recherches sur le Caoutchouc au Cambodge; IRCC) at Chup and to the adjacent French rubber plantation (Compagnie du Cambodge). At IRCC we examined Institute records and interviewed the following professional staff:

Dr. W. L. Resing (chemist) (Director)
M. Gilbert Deconinck (plant pathologist)
M. Chai Kim Chun (biochemist)
M. Langlois (agronomist)
M. Tupy (plant physiologist)

We visited the adjacent plantation (the second largest in the world) in order to become acquainted with healthy rubber trees of the several major varieties at various ages.

Saturday, 27 December 1969. Visit to a moderately damaged, medium-sized, private (cooperative) plantation at Chipeang (just east of Krek) (employing *ca.* 500 workers), and to the associated village (population *ca.* 1,500). This was a typical (though somewhat larger) example of the many small plantations in the region that were damaged to a greater or lesser extent. We inspected the damage and interviewed M. Buoy San, the director, as well as several tappers and villagers at random.

Next, we visited the heavily damaged, large, private plantation at Dar (Société Khmère d'Hévéaculture de Dar; SKHD) in the company of Dr. Resing and M. Deconinck of IRCC. Here we also inspected the damage and interviewed M. Som Khom, the director, as well as several field foremen and tappers.

Monday, 29 December 1969. Visit to the rather heavily damaged, large French plantation at Mimot (Société des Plantations Réunies de Mimot; SPRM) which employs some 15,000 workers. Here we inspected the damage and interviewed:

M. E. Pellegrin (Director General)

M. C. Audureau (Assistant Director)

Dr. Charles Bosquet (M.D.; Director of the hospital at Mimot)

as well as the five Cambodian owners of five very small nearby rubber plantations (and each living in a different nearby village).

Next, we visited a small village in the vicinity (Chalang III) to inspect in some detail the damage done to local agricultural and horticultural crops and to interview the inhabitants.

Observations and Findings

General. The principal period of herbicidal application seems to have occurred during April and the early part of May of 1969, and thus at the end of the dry, dormant season. Our observations were therefore carried out some eight months later and after the passing of one complete growing season (the wet monsoon season of May through November). The U.S. State Department examination had been made about two months after spraying, shortly after the onset of the growing season.

About 70,000 hectares (173,000 acres) were damaged, of which about 10,000 hectares (24,700 acres) were damaged rather heavily. This affected area contains about 15,500 hectares (38,300 acres) of damaged rubber plantations, of which about 6,000 hectares (14,800 acres) were damaged rather heavily. Of the 15,500 hectares of damaged rubber, about 11,400 hectares (28,200 acres) are over 6-7 years old and thus in production.

The herbicides used seemed to have been restricted to a mixture of 2,4-dichlorophenoxyacetic acid (2,4-D) and 2,4,5-trichlorophenoxyacetic acid (2,4,5-T) in oil soluble formulations; this mixture goes under the U.S. Defense Department code name "Orange." We concluded that it was agent Orange because of the characteristic, dramatic and selective effects of this hormonal class of herbicides; and because the essentially normal growth of the subsequently planted garden crops precluded the other more persistent agents also used by the U.S. armed forces. The severity and selectivity of injury suggested applications in the approximate range of 0.5 to 3 kilograms per hectare (0.4-3 pounds/acre) of active herbicidal ingredients. The lesser amount refers to the eastern and western portions of the affected area, the greater amount to the central portion.

The herbicidal mixture that was presumably used is highly (though somewhat variably) toxic to a wide range of dicotyledonous annuals and perennials, both herbaceous and woody (including rubber, numerous fruit, and some timber trees and many vegetables). It is generally less toxic to monocotyledonous plants (including rice and other cereals, bamboo, banana, and palms). Both 2,4-D and 2,4,5-T are toxic to lethal by virtue of being absorbed and translocated by the vegetation, thence to mimic certain natural endogenous growth hormones. They cause erratic and uncontrolled overgrowth, flower, fruit, and leaf abscission, branch dieback, temporary sterility, and other ill effects; and in some instances death. Any 2,4-D that reaches the ground decomposes within a few weeks after application, and 2,4,5-T within a few months.

Damage to rubber trees. Highly accurate damage estimates can be made with respect to rubber (*Hevea brasiliensis*) since very precise records are kept by the IRCC and the larger plantations on a variety by variety and block by block basis with respect to tree growth, tree health, latex yield, and latex quality. The managerial plantation personnel are well trained and competent, and the methods employed by them are scientifically and technologically up to date. Latex yield per hectare in this region is the highest in the world.

Although quite a number of varieties (clones *sensu stricto*) are in use in Cambodia, more than 90% of all commercial production is more or less equally based upon three major varieties: "GT.1," "PR.107," and "PB.86." (The U.S. State Department report describes the three major varieties to be AVROS.50, which apparently has been confused with GT.1; PR.107; and PB.36, which is apparently a misprint of PB.86.)

GT.1, originally defoliated 90-100%, has since experienced the greatest amount of branch dieback, and has been the slowest to recover. Branch dieback of 2-3 meters (7-10 feet) or more was quite common. Young trees of this variety and those growing under adverse soil conditions have in many instances died over the past eight months. Latex production in the half year following spraying was reduced by as much as 70-80% in this variety. The current complement of leaves is somewhat abnormal in appearance and the dry rubber content (DRC) of the latex now flowing is subnormal.

PR.107 has turned out to be somewhat less sensitive than GT.1, all of the above described effects having occurred to a somewhat lesser degree. PB.86 was least affected by the herbicides and has now after one growing season recovered to a large extent.

Over-all, the IRCC has determined conservatively that the May to November 1969 latex production of the sprayed rubber trees was reduced by an average of 35-40%. This represents an economic loss so far of approximately U.S. $11.0 million. We judge these figures to be reliable since we were impressed by the detail and accuracy of the records kept by the IRCC and the larger plantations and by the obvious competence and integrity of the professional personnel involved. It should be added that this opinion was shared by the U.S. State Department team that had made the earlier inspection. It is also important to note that the damaged rubber trees in production represent over one-third of all the rubber trees currently in production in Cambodia. Rubber is the first or second most important export commodity of the nation, crucial to its balance of trade.

It is difficult to accurately estimate the entire extent of present and future damage since many direct and indirect factors are involved. Whereas PB.86 may be back to essentially normal production within another year, GT.1 may well level off at only 80% of normal production within another two or three years. Presumably, PR.107 will be intermediate in its rate of recovery. The death of some GT.1 and PR.107 trees will preclude full recovery of normal production per hectare until their normal time of replacement at about age 40-50. (The larger plantations have trees in blocks of about 100 hectares [250 acres] in all age classes, and follow a regular annual schedule of renewal.)

One of the serious indirect problems that has already resulted from the herbicidal defoliation is the production of a luxuriant understory of weeds throughout the affected area, resulting from greatly increased illumination of the forest floor. These weeds not only compete for the limited soil nutrients and water, but also enormously increase the fire hazard during the dry season. Indeed, we inspected the disastrous results of one 23-hectare (57-acre) fire resulting from just this situation, all the rubber trees having been killed. These weeds are being cut in part, but financial limitations preclude adequate control. The weed-associated losses may well approach the magnitude of the losses resulting from the drop in latex production.

Another problem (which applies most seriously to the many small plantations and to the entirely damaged larger ones) results from the fact that tapping of the injured trees must often be continued almost unabated for pressing financial and social reasons. Most of the families comprising the *ca.* 30,000 inhabitants of the affected area depend upon tapping as their prime source of income. This unfortunate situation prevents the injured trees from recovering as rapidly as they might if they were left alone for a year or two, and is likely to lead to an increased rate of mortality. Moreover, since the tappers are paid on the basis of amount of latex collected daily, they are currently earning minimal wages.

Many of the blocks established during the past several years were decimated regardless of variety, so that the larger plantations in the affected area will largely lack these several age classes. This and the possible need for earlier replacement of mature blocks (owing to possible earlier senility, *i.e.,* earlier drop in latex production) will unbalance the normal rotational cycles for decades to come. An added aggravation is that some of the budwood gardens (the source of the cion material for the reestablishment of the clonal varieties) were badly damaged.

The dead branch stubs and the weakened condition of the trees may reslt in future increases in fungal or insect depredations, although there are as yet no indications of this.

Finally, it is of physiological interest to note that a very high proportion of two rubber varieties, TR.1600 and BD.5, have died during the interval since the spraying. It is most fortunate that these two highly sensitive varieties are essentially not in commercial use in the affected area.

Damage to other vegetation. A large variety of garden crops (both agricultural and horticultural) were devastated in the seemingly endless number of small villages scattered throughout the affected area. Virtually all of the *ca.* 30,000 local inhabitants are subsistence farmers that depend for their wellbeing upon their own local produce. These people saw their crops then growing literally wither before their eyes. Indeed, it was the widespread death of the vegetables that heralded the rest of the damage to the area. Their then current crops of vegetables of numerous kinds, of pineapples (*Ananas comosus*), of guavas (*Psidium guajava*), of jack fruit (*Artocarpus integra*), of papayas (*Carica papaya*), and of many, many more were simply destroyed.

Some of the other more important food crops that were largely wiped out at the time included durian (*Durio zibethimus*), manioc (*Manihot esculenta* and *M. ultissima*), tomato (*Lycopersicum esculentum*), several types of beans (*Phaseolus vulgaris, Glycine max, Vigna sesquipedales,* etc.), cauliflower (*Brassica oleracea*), and custard apple (*Annona diversifolia? reticulata?*).

Food plants that seemed to be only little or moderately damaged by the herbicides included taro (*Colocasia esculentum*), ginger (*Zingiber officinale*), banana (*Musa sapietum,* etc.), orange (*Citrus sinensis*), longan (*Nephelium longana*), mango (*Mangifera indica*), sapodilla (*Achras zapota*), sugar palm (*Borassus flabellifera*), and coconut (*Cocos nucifera*). Of these, coconut is now showing a moderate measure of delayed injury not originally expected. A number of annual crops were largely spared because for the most part they had not yet been planted. Rice (*Oryza sativa*), although moderately resistant to the herbicides, falls into this category.

At the time of our visit, the annual plants that had been planted subsequent to the spraying for the most part seemed to be normal in appearance. On the other hand, pineapple plants look healthy but are to date refusing to bear. The new papaya crop is small and the fruits and leaves are somewhat distorted on a number of the plants. Some guava trees have died in the interim, and none of those that have persisted are as yet bearing. The custard apples are for the most part not yet bearing either. Lychee trees (*Litchie chinensis*), apparently not an important crop locally, suffered severe dieback and are not yet bearing. The important jack fruit trees (anticipated by the U.S. State Department team to largely recover) are unfortunately now for the most part dead. Indeed, the dead jack fruit trees stand as grim reminders of the "poison from the sky" beside virtually every home in the area. (The Cambodian Ministry of Agriculture estimates that some 45,000 of these were killed or severely damaged.) The banana plants seem completely normal again and the manioc trees seem to be recovering well (although some of the new fruits are abnormal in shape).

Kapok trees (*Ceiba pentandra*), whose fibers provide a small cash crop for the local inhabitants, were largely killed in village after village. The few surviving trees are not yet bearing their fiber-producing fruits. We inspected two small plantations in the area, one of coffee (*Coffea arabica*) and another of teak (*Tectona grandis*), neither of which seemed to have been damaged by the herbicides.

The forested portions between the plantations and villages in the affected area presently support only a scattering of commercially usable timber trees of a variety of species. Although many of the few tall timber trees had been initially defoliated, most now seem to be slowly recovering (largely through the production of adventitious shoots). We did observe some dead individuals of two commercial species of dipterocarp: lumbor (*Shorea hypochra*) and phdiec (*Anisoptera cochinchinensis*).

Damages to crops other than rubber have been estimated by the Cambodian Ministry of Agriculture to amount to approximately U.S. $1.2 million. The extent of privation caused the local inhabitants cannot be estimated.

Damage to land and soil. We observed no evidence of increased erosion or of soil hardening via laterization and no evidence of change in the level of the water table or of any other physiographic factor. Nor did we find any evidence of weather modification.

Damage to livestock and other animals. All of our interviews with the local inhabitants consistently disclosed that village livestock became ill for a period of several days soon after spraying. Whereas the larger animals (water buffaloes, cattle, and mature pigs and sheep) became only mildly ill and all recovered, some of the smaller ones (chickens, ducks, and young pigs) suffered more severely and in some cases were reported to have died. The domestic mammals were described as having had digestive problems, whereas the domestic birds became partially paralyzed for a time. Apparently many wild birds became similarly disabled and could be captured easily. There were also a number of small dead birds found at the time in the woods and fields.

It is interesting to note here that eastern Cambodia in general has experienced quite a substantial increase in a variety of wildlife, apparently driven out of Vietnam by the defoliation and other ravages of the war. Included are muntjacs and other species of deer, wild cattle (gaurs, bantengs, and some koupreys), elephants, a number of monkey species, and wild pigs.

Effect on humans. Many of the local inhabitants we interviewed spoke of widespread temporary diarrhea and vomiting, particularly among infants and to a lesser extent among the general adult populace. At one location (Chipeang) water was trucked in for a time following spraying to provide uncontaminated water for the children. In those instances where the people depended largely upon deep wells for their water supply we received no report of human digestive problems.

We had a lengthy interview with the physician who directs a hospital in the affected area (at Mimot) that serves some 15,000 people, and which handles about 200 local patients a day. (The doctor speaks not only French and English, but Cambodian and Vietnamese as well.) We also inspected his detailed hospital patient records for 1968 and 1969. This investigation revealed no increase in the incidence of any malady during or subsequent to spraying. Owing to the known abortive and teratogenic effects of 2,4,5-T in laboratory animals and its similar suspected effects amongst the South Vietnamese population, we gave particular attention to this possibility. However, there has been no increase discernible in recent months. (There are about fifty local births per month and the birth of one malformed infant about every two months.)

Source of the Herbicidal Spray

There is, of course, no question that the responsibility for the extensive herbicidal damage we have observed in Cambodia rests upon the United States. Only the United States has the ability and matériel locally to carry out such operations. By its own admission, the United States has in South Vietnam carried out extensive aerial spraying with a variety of herbicides. Indeed, over 10% of the entire surface of South Vietnam has been heavily sprayed over the past eight years. The U.S. State Department report enumerates the spray missions in some detail that were carried out in the neighboring Tay Ninh province of South Vietnam between March and June of 1969.

Some of the Cambodian damage, perhaps as much as one-third of it, certainly appears to be the result of drift from some of these operations. Indeed, such drift is unavoidable given the type of herbicide used, the method of application, and the existing topographical and meteorological conditions.

Although denied by the U.S. Defense Department, the U.S. State Department report concluded that a significant portion of the damage was virtually certain to be the result of direct overflight. We have concluded even less ambiguously that the evidence for direct overflight is incontrovertible. The total amount of damage, the areal extent of damage, the distance of damage from the South Vietnamese operations, the prevailing wind direction during the period in question, and the spatial pattern of severity (in the central portion of the affected area severity essentially the same near the border as 18 kilometers [11 miles] in) have forced us to the conclusion that at least two-thirds of the actual damage in Cambodia was the result of direct overflight. Moreover, a number of the local inhabitants we interviewed reported to have seen spray planes in operation overhead. M. Buoy San, director of the plantation at Chipeang, described to us a low-flying plane spraying his plantation at about 9 A.M. on three separate occasions in April and May.

Some 70,000 hectares (173,000 acres) were at least slightly injured. If one makes the conservative assumption that this entire area was damaged by a dose rate averaging as little as 0.5 kg/hectare (0.4 pound/acre) of active herbicide, a total application of some 35,000 kilograms (77,000 pounds) would have been needed. How much of this could have resulted from drift over the border arising from the U.S. military operations in adjacent South Vietnam?

Each spray plane carries a payload of about 3,600 kilograms (7,900 pounds) of active herbicide. If one can assume that no more than about 10% of the herbicide in each aircraft could have drifted onto the affected area, this would mean that of the order of 100 planes had to have been flying missions rather near to the Cambodian border during April and early May of 1969. Actually (according to the U.S. State Department report) only about half that number of planes flew defoliation missions in the adjacent Tay Ninh province during that time. Moreover, meteorological conditions and other considerations led the U.S. State Department team to conclude that drift could only have originated from five missions apparently totalling 29 planes.

Thus, even assuming a conservative over-all average dose rate of 0.5 kg/hectare (0.4 pound/acre), drift could have accounted for as much as one-third of the total injury that occurred. Our examination of the affected area suggested that its eastern and western portions may have received about 0.5 kg/hectare. However, there is a large central block of perhaps 10,000 hectares (24,700 acres) in which the extent and selectivity of damage suggests a fairly uniform application rate of the order of 2-3 kg/hectare (2-3 pounds/acre). This more heavily damaged zone extends about 20 kilometers (12 miles) from north to south and about 5 kilometers (3 miles) from east to west. It includes the rubber plantations at Dar, Chalang, and Prek Chhlong. The damage on this central block can only be explained on the basis of a direct overflight. It could be accounted for by some seven planes flying at a higher than usual altitude.

We conclude that it is highly likely that the overflights were a deliberate violation of the frontier.* The border is recognizable from the air and both United States air and ground forces seem to be intimately familiar with its location. Although U.S. aircraft violate Cambodian territory daily for purposes of reconnaissance, the daily military combat activities in the region (a number of which we observed at rather close hand) are for the most part strictly limited to the South Vietnamese side. The fact that rubber plantations (which are readily distinguishable from the air) were so heavily hit (one-third of all of this major Cambodian crop), suggests an attempt at punitive action on the part of the United States. That U.S. pilots are, we are told, under routine standing orders in South Vietnam to avoid the spraying of rubber adds further support to the hypothesis that this particular action was deliberate.

Conclusion

Our mission was a sad one, a mission whose raison d'être we wish had never occurred. The loss in rubber production will be relatively easy to ascertain over the next year or two, and restitution will hopefully be made by the United States. (We concur with the U.S. State Department report that a fairly reliable evaluation of damages should be possible following one more growing season, *i.e.,* toward the end of 1970; we concur with the Cambodian Ministry of Agriculture report that an economist should be included in the next visiting team.) The damages to rubber that we have observed are certain to result in a significant setback in Cambodia's slow but promising struggle to strengthen its economy. Therefore, the sooner the United States makes restitution the better.

---

* On 18 December 1969, Mr. Thomas R. Pickering, Deputy Director of the Bureau of Politico-Military Affairs of the U.S. Department of State, in testimony before the House Subcommittee on National Security Policy and Scientific Developments (published by the Committee on Foreign Affairs in early 1970) admitted "that the greatest part of the damage was caused by a deliberate and direct overflight of the rubber plantations."

We feel particularly grieved about the innumerable direct and indirect losses suffered by the innocent local populace. The extent of these losses can never be determined satisfactorily and will never be compensated adequately. We have seen at first hand how particularly drastic this type of military action is for people whose very existence is so closely tied to the land.

Cambodia is a small nation attempting to remain neutral between East and West and to remain at peace with its neighbors despite enormous external pressures from all quarters. We cannot understand and we cannot condone the violations of Cambodian territory by the United States, for which the present report furnishes but one example. Despite a week of free and unhampered travel by automobile, on foot, and by low-flying aircraft along hundreds of kilometers of the border, we could find no evidence of Viet Cong activity in Cambodia; nor did our repeated conversations with Cambodians and Europeans living along the border suggest any such activity.

We therefore urge that the United States adopt an ironclad policy of respect for the rights of the Khmer people and of the Royal Cambodian Government. Only in this way will we be able to bolster the deteriorating amity between the United States and Cambodia, so important in these times of international disharmony.

Finally, we cannot help but mention the United States herbicidal activities in neighboring South Vietnam. We have witnessed the devastation caused by this relatively minor incursion into Cambodia. How much worse it must be for the hapless peoples of South Vietnam whose lands are being sprayed so much more heavily and systematically. Theirs is a long-term legacy of economic and ecological devastation whose full enormity is difficult to grasp.

MILITARY USE OF HERBICIDES:
SOME AVAILABLE LITERATURE

Army, U.S. Dept. of (1969)
EMPLOYMENT OF RIOT CONTROL AGENTS,
FLAME, SMOKE, ANTIPLANT AGENTS, AND PER-
SONNEL DETECTORS IN COUNTERGUERRILLA OP-
ERATIONS.
U.S. Dept. Army Trng. Circ. TC 3-16, 85 pp (pp. 62-68;
80-81).

Fair, S. D. (1963)
NO PLACE TO HIDE: HOW DEFOLIANTS EXPOSE
THE VIET CONG.
Army 14(2):54-55 [also: Armed Forces Chemical Jour.
18(1):5-6.]

House, W. B. et al. (1967)
ASSESSMENT OF ECOLOGICAL EFFECTS OF EX-
TENSIVE OR REPEATED USE OF HERBICIDES.
U.S. Dept. Defense, DDC AD824314, 369 pp. [the "MRI"
report].

Huddle, F. P. (1969)
TECHNOLOGY ASSESSMENT OF THE VIETNAM
DEFOLIANT MATTER: A CASE HISTORY.
U.S. House Repres., Comm. on Science & Astronautics,
73 pp.

McCarthy, R. D. (1969)
ULTIMATE FOLLY: WAR BY PESTILENCE, AS-
PHYXIATION AND DEFOLIATION.
N.Y.: Knopf, 176 pp. (pp. 74-98).

Mrak, E. M. et al. (1969)
REPORT OF THE SECRETARY'S COMMISSION ON PESTICIDES AND THEIR RELATIONSHIP TO ENVIRONMENTAL HEALTH.
U.S. Dept. Health, Education, & Welfare, 677 pp.

Rose, S. (ed.) (1969)
CBW: CHEMICAL AND BIOLOGICAL WARFARE.
Boston: Beacon, 209 pp. (pp. 62-98).

Scientific Research (1969)
MISSION TO VIETNAM. [Interview with E. W. Pfeiffer & G. H. Orians]
Scientific Research [†] 4(12):22-30; (13):26-30; (15):5.

Tschirley, F. H. (1968)
RESEARCH REPORT: RESPONSE OF TROPICAL AND SUBTROPICAL WOODY PLANTS TO CHEMICAL TREATMENTS.
U.S. Agricultural Research Serv., Publ. CR-13-67, 197 pp.

Tschirley, F. H. (1969)
DEFOLIATION IN VIETNAM.
Science 163:779-786.

Westing, A. H. et al. (1970)
REPORT ON HERBICIDAL DAMAGE BY THE UNITED STATES IN SOUTH-EASTERN CAMBODIA.
U.S. Congressional Record 116: [in press].

STATEMENT OF
DR. SAMUEL S. EPSTEIN, CHILDREN'S CANCER RESEARCH FOUNDATION, INC., AND HARVARD MEDICAL SCHOOL, BOSTON, MASSACHUSETTS

Before the Subcommittee on Energy,
Natural Resources, and the Environment
of the Senate Committee on Commerce

———

April 14, 1970

The subject of my presentation today is teratogenic effects of 2,4,5-T formulations.

A. Teratogenicity as a Public Health Hazard

Potential hazards posed by environmental pollutants and drugs include toxicity or poisoning, carcinogenicity or induction of cancer, mutagenicity or induction of genetic damage, and teratogenicity or induction of developmental abnormalities in the growing embryo. Although teratogenic effects of various agents have been recognized for several decades, it was only as a reaction to the thalidomide episode of 1962 that a requirement for teratogenicity data became established.

Teratology is the study of congenital malformations. These are generally defined as structural abnormalities which can be recognized at or shortly after birth and which can cause disability or death. Less restrictedly, teratology also includes microscopical, biochemical and functional abnormalities of prenatal origin.

Congenital malformations pose incalculable personal, familial, and social stresses. The financial cost to society of one severely retarded child, computed on the basis of specialized training and custodial care alone, approximates to $250,000;[1] this figure excludes further costs to society due to deprivation of earnings. In the absence of a comprehensive national surveillance system, the precise overall incidence of congenital malformations is unknown; this incidence has been variously estimated as ranging between 3-4% of total live births.

Three major categories of human teratogens have been identified—viral infections, *eg.,* German measles, irradiation, *eg.,* X-rays, and chemical agents, *eg.,* thalidomide and mercury.

B. Methods for Teratogenicity Testing

Teratogenic effects of chemicals and other agents should of course be identified in experimental animals, rather than in human beings following accidental or unrecognized exposure. Test agents should be administered to pregnant animals during active organogenesis of their developing embryos. Shortly before anticipated birth, embryos should be harvested by caesarean section and examined. Parameters to be considered in test and concurrent control animals should include the incidence of abnormal litters, the incidence of abnormal fetuses *per* litter, the incidence of specific congenital abnormalities, the incidence of fetal mortality, maternal weight gains in pregnancy, and maternal and fetal organ/body weight ratios. Additionally, some pregnant animals should be allowed to give birth in order to identify abnormalities that may otherwise manifest only in the perinatal period.

Agents and their known metabolites should be administered to two or more mammalian species, under various nutritional conditions, during active organogenesis, and by a variety of routes reflecting possible human exposure. Of interest in this

---

[1] Oberle, M. W. *Science 165,* 991–992, 1969.

connection is the lack of data in the available literature on teratogenicity testing by the respiratory route; respiratory exposure is particularly important for pesticide aerosols and vapors. Agents should be tested at higher dose levels than might be anticipated in humans following high level accidental exposure, as well as following extensive low level exposure. This is essential to attempt to reduce the insensitivity of conventional test systems, based on very small numbers of animals, compared with the millions of humans at presumptive risk. To illustrate this further, let us assume that at actual human exposure levels, a pesticide induces teratogenic effects or cancer in as many as 1 out of 10,000 humans, then the chances of detecting this in test groups of less than 50 rats or mice exposed at these actual levels would be very low. Indeed, many more than 10,000 rats or mice, depending on their spontaneous incidence of teratogenic effects or cancer, would be required to demonstrate a statistically significant effect, if we assumed that rats and humans have similar sensitivity to the teratogen or carcinogen being studied. For some teratogens, humans may be less or may be more sensitive than test animals. Meclizine for example, is teratogenic in the rat, but not apparently in a restricted number of humans studied.[2,3] With thalidomide conversely, the lowest effective human teratogenic dose is 0.5 mg/kg/day; corresponding values for the mouse, rat, dog, and hamster are 30, 50, 100 and 350 mg/kg/day.[4] Thus, humans are 60 times more sensitive than mice, 100 times more sensitive than rats, 200 times more sensitive than dogs, and 700 times more sensitive than hamsters. Clearly, attempts to determine a safe level for thalidomide, based on animal teratogenicity data, would clearly expose humans to significant teratogenic hazards. Accordingly, it is routine practice to test for terato-

[2] King, C. *J. Pharm. Exp. Therap. 147,* 391, 1965.
[3] Yerushalamy, J. and Milkovich, L. *Am. J. Obs. Gynae., 93,* 553, 1965.
[4] Kalter, H. Teratology of the central nervous system, *University of Chicago Press,* 1968.

genicity and carcinogenicity at a range of concentrations, including those higher than human exposure levels, and extending to maximally tolerated doses (MTD). Even at MTD levels administered to mice from day 7 of life until sacrifice at 18 months, less than 10% of the 140 pesticides tested in the recent Bionetics study were shown to be carcinogenic.

The report of the Advisory Panel on Teratogenicity states unambiguously . . . "Pesticides should be tested at various concentrations including levels substantially higher than those to which the human population are likely to be exposed." The report also emphasizes the insensitivity of standard test systems imposed by the relatively insufficient numbers of litters conventionally tested. The report further states . . . "Thus, compounds showing no increase (in birth defects) cannot be considered non-teratogenic."

Epidemiological surveys of human populations may provide *post hoc* information on geographical or temporal clusters of unusual types or frequencies of malformations following exposure to undetected or untested teratogens in the environment. However, logistic considerations, quite apart from inadequate current surveillance systems, limit the utility of this approach. It should be emphasized that no major known human teratogen, such as X-rays, German measles, mercury, or thalidomide, has been identified by retrospective epidemiological analyses, even in industrialized countries with highly evolved and sophisticated medical facilities. Prospective epidemiologic surveys on agents previously shown or suspected to be teratogenic, by experimental studies or by retrospective population surveys, are clearly inappropriate.

C. Bionetics Studies on Teratogenicity of 2,4,5-T

Bionetics Research Laboratories, Inc., of Litton Industries, under a contract from the National Cancer Institute, tested

48 pesticides, including 2,4,5-T, and related compounds, for teratogenic effects during 1965–68. Although the Bionetics studies were originally designed for purposes of large-scale screening, 2,4,5-T was tested more extensively than any other pesticide. Thus, the data on 2,4,5-T may be regarded as more definitive. . . .

2,4,5-T was tested on repeated occasions from 1965–1968 in 3 strains of mice and in one strain of rats by subcutaneous and/or oral administration, over a dose range from 4.6–113 mg/kg. The total numbers of litters tested at each dose level, by each route in all strains and species (excluding C_3H mice in which only 1 litter was tested) were as follows:

Test Animals	Dose mg/kg	Number of Litters in Test Groups	
		Oral	Subcutaneous
BL6 mice	21.5	—	6
	46.4	6	—
	113.0	12	35
BL6/AK mice	113.0	—	13
AK mice	113.0	7	14
Sprague Dawley rats	4.6	8	—
	10.0	7	—
	21.5	8	—
	46.4	8	—

As can be seen, the bulk of the data was obtained with BL6 mice. Due to control variability, the BL6 data have been considered for 3 time intervals—prior to September 1966; from September to November 1966; and from November 1966 to August 1968. Data on AK mice were considered for 2 time intervals—prior to November 1966; and from November 1966 to August 1968. Data for BL6 mice, AK mice, and Sprague Dawley rats, as derived from the Bionetics report, are as follows:

BL6 Mice: 2,4,5-T administered on days 6–14 or days 9–17, and mice sacrificed on day 18 of pregnancy.

	% Abnormal Fetuses				
	Subcutaneous administration				Oral administration
Dose mg/kg	Prior to Sept. '66	Sept.– Nov. '66	Nov. '66– Aug. '68	Un- dated	Nov. '66–Aug. '68
21.5	7	—	—	—	—
46.4	—	—	—	—	37*
113.0 (1)	—	74*	31	—	67*
113.0 (2)	—	—	26*	—	—
113.0 (3)	—	—	—	78*	—

* Statistically significant increase compared with controls

BL6/AK Mice: 2,4,5-T administered on days 6–14, and mice sacrificed on day 18 of pregnancy.

Subcutaneous Dose, mg/kg	% Abnormal fetuses
113.0	39*

* Statistically significant increase compared with controls

AK Mice: 2,4,5-T administered from days 6–15, and mice sacrificed on day 19 of pregnancy.

Dose mg/kg	% Abnormal Fetuses		
	Subcutaneous administration		Oral administration
	Prior to Nov. '66	Nov. '66– Aug. '68	Nov. '66–Aug. '68
113.0	31*	36*	49*

* Statistically significant increase compared with controls

Sprague Dawley Rats: 2,4,5-T administered from days 10–15, and rats sacrificed on day 20 of pregnancy.

Oral Dose mg/kg	% Abnormal Fetuses
4.6	39*
10.0	78*
21.5 (1)	90*
21.5 (2)	92
46.4 (1)	100*
46.6 (2)	75

* Statistically significant increase compared with controls

Major abnormalities in mice were cleft palates and cystic kidneys, and in rats, cystic kidneys and gastro-intestinal haemorrhages. Increased fetal mortality was generally concomitant with these abnormalities. It is of particular interest that 39% abnormal embryos with cystic kidneys were seen in rats even at the lowest dose tested. Thus, the *no effect* level was not reached even at 4.6 mg/kg.

Teratogenicity data on 2,4,5-T, as summarized in the Bionetics report, are quoted *in extenso* opposite. Some critical sentences are italicized:

This compound was given by the oral route to BL6 mice at dosages of 46.6 and 113 mg/kg and to AKR mice at 113 mg/kg. It was given by subcutaneous injection to BL6 mice at dosages of 21.5 and 113 mg/kg and to AKR mice and B6AK hybrids at 113 mg/kg. It was also given subcutaneously to C₃H mice at 215 mg/kg, but there were too few of these to merit inclusion in the discussion which follows. Administration was for eight days (6th through 14th) in most cases; for nine days (6th through 15th) in some; and for five days (10th through 14th) in one case—the details are indicated in the tabulated results. Subcutaneous administration used DMSO as a vehicle; oral used 50% honey.

With the single exception of the lowest dosage used (21.5 mg/kg to BL6 subcutaneously) all dosages, routes, and strains resulted in increased incidence of abnormal fetuses. The incidence of cleft palate was high at the 113 mg/kg dosage, but not at lower levels. The incidence of cystic kidney was also high except in the AKR strain and in the BL6 mice which received 46.4 mg/kg orally. Fetal mortality was increased in all groups given 113 mg/kg for eight or nine days, but not in mice (BL6) given this dosage for only five days nor in the two groups of BL6 mice given lesser dosages (46.4 mg/kg orally and 21.5 mg/kg subcutaneously).

Most fetal and maternal measurements showed inconsistent changes from which no conclusions can be drawn. In contrast, there was a highly consistent decrease in maternal weight gain in BL6 mice given 113 mg/kg by either route. Lower dosages and the AKR strain showed either no change or a slight increase. All dosages, strains, and routes showed an increase in the maternal liver weight and this led to a further study discussed separately below.

These results imply a hazard of teratogenesis in the use of this compound. The problems of extrapolation preclude definition of the hazard on the basis of these studies, but its existence seems clear.

The observed influence of 2,4,5-T on maternal liver weight as mentioned above raised a question as to its effect on the fetal liver. This was answered by a study carried out in BL6 mice using subcutaneous injections of DMSO solutions at a dosage of 113 mg/kg only. The period of administration was lengthened to cover the period from the 9th through 17th day of gestation. Separate control groups were used concurrently. Except for the inclusion of fetal liver weight, measurements were made as previously described.

The fetal livers of the 2,4,5-T treated mice weighed significantly more than those of controls given DMSO only and the weights of the whole fetuses were significantly less. Correspondingly, there was an increase in the fetal liver weight expressed as percent of body weight.

Other observations were consistent with those reported above. The incidence of abnormal fetuses was unusually high as were those of cleft palate and cystic kidney.

Because of the potential importance of the findings in mice, an additional study was carried out in rats of the Sprague-Dawley strain. Using dosages of 21.5 and 46.4 mg/kg suspended in 50% honey and given by the oral route on the 6th through 15th days of gestation, we observed excessive fetal mortality (almost 80%) and a high incidence of abnormalities in the survivors. When the beginning of administration was delayed until the 10th day, fetal mortality was somewhat less, but still quite high even when dosage was reduced to 4.6 mg/kg. *The incidence of abnormal fetuses was threefold that in controls even with the smallest dosage and shortest period used.* Fetal and maternal measurements showed only occasional instances of significant differences from controls except in the case of maternal liver weight which was consistently increased in all 2,4,5-T treated animals.

It seems inescapable that 2,4,5-T is teratogenic in this strain of rats when given orally at the dosage schedules used here. These findings lend emphasis to the hazard implied by the results of studies on mice.

D. Recent Re-analysis of the Bionetics Data on Teratogenicity of 2,4,5-T

More refined and more appropriate additional statistical analyses of these data were presented and discussed in the report of the Advisory Panel on Teratogenicity of Pesticides. These are *clearly confirmatory* of the original conclusions of the Bionetics report on the teratogenicity of 2,4,5-T. Some relevant portions of the HEW panel report are quoted *in extenso* below:

Tested more extensively than other pesticides, 2,4,5-T was clearly teratogenic as evidenced by production of statistically increased proportions of litters affected, and increased proportions of abnormal fetuses within litters in both DMSO and Honey for both 157BL/6 and AKR mice. In particular, cleft palate and cystic kidneys were significantly more prevalent. In addition, a hybrid strain resulting from a C57BL/6 female and AKR male showed significant increases in anomalies, in particular cystic kidney, when administered at 113 mg/kg of body weight in DMSO.

Additionally, 2,4,5-T was tested in Sprague-Dawley rats. When given orally at dosages of 4.6, 10.0 and 46.4 mg/kg on days 10 through 15 of gestation, an excessive fetal mortality, up to 60 percent at the highest dose, and high incidence of abnormalities in the survivors was obtained. *The incidence of fetuses with kidney anomalies was three-fold that of the controls, even with the smallest dosage tested.*

E. Recent Studies on Teratogenicity Testing of Relatively Pure 2,4,5-T

In view of the fact that the Bionetics study was conducted with a sample of 2,4,5-T which was subsequently shown to contain a relatively high concentration, 27 *ppm,* of a tetrachloro dioxin contaminant, testing has been recently repeated with relatively pure samples containing less than 1 *ppm* of this particular dioxin. The results of these studies were presented at a recent conference of 2/24/70 at the FDA; the Dow Chemical Co. data were presented at the 9th annual meeting of the Society of Toxicology, Atlanta, 3/17/70. *As can be seen from the data summarized below, purified 2,4,5-T is teratogenic in three species—rats, mice, and hamsters.* These data should be regarded as preliminary. Data on chickens and eggs will not be presented here or subsequently.

1. Dow Chemical Co. Studies[5] (*Society of Toxicology meetings 3/17/70*)

2,4,5-T with 0.5 *ppm* dioxins, as a probable contaminant, was tested in pregnant rats by repeated oral administration at doses of 1, 3, 6, 12, and 24 mg/kg; the maximal dose tested was 24 mg/kg. No embryo deaths or weight losses were noted within the dose range tested. However, at 24 mg/kg there was a 7-fold increase in the incidence of fetuses with defective ossification of the 5th sternebra; poor sternebral ossification was noted in 4/103 control fetuses, and in 29/103 fetuses of 2,4,5-T treated groups.

Defective sternebral ossification has been described in the rat as an expression of the teratogenic effects of drugs such as protamine zinc insulin and tolbutamide.[6, 7]

2. NIEHS Studies (*FDA Conference, 2/24/70*)

Using the purest sample of 2,4,5-T, made available by Dow Chemical Co., teratogenic effects were induced in Swiss-Webster mice. Cleft palates were noted at dose levels of 150 mg/kg and scattered abnormalities at 100 mg/kg; the cleft palate incidence in control mice was essentially zero.

3. FDA Studies (*FDA Conference, 2/24/70*)

Hamsters were injected with 5 doses of 100 mg/kg/day of various batches of purified 2,4,5-T between days 6–10 of pregnancy. In one of these studies, there was a 66% incidence of mortality in 50 fetuses. Of the surviving fetuses, 17% had congenital abnormalities—crooked tail, missing limb, and defect in skull fusion. No data were presented on possible effects induced by doses less than 100 mg/kg.

---

[5] Emerson, J. L., Thompson, D. J., Gerbig, C. G., Robinson, V. B. (Dow Chemical Co.), Teratogenic study of 2,4,5-Trichlorophenoxy acetic acid in the rat. Society of Toxicology, 9th Annual Meeting, Atlanta, Georgia 3/17/70.

[6] Lichtenstein, H., Guest, G. M. and Warkany, J. *Proc. Soc. Exp. Biol. & Med. 78*, 398–402, 1951.

[7] Dawson, J. E. *Diabetes 13*, 527–531, 1964.

Of additional interest was a report also presented at the same conference on purified 2,4-D, which produced a 22% incidence of congenital abnormalities in hamsters at a dose level of 100 mg/kg/day.

F. Toxicity of Dioxins

Rabbit ear skin is highly sensitive to dioxins, repeated application of which can produce chloracne, as a cumulative manifestation of local toxicity. Approximately 0.3 μg of the tetra isomer will produce a positive response; "> 10 μg on a (surface) wipe sample indicates acute hazard[8] (to man)."

The acute oral LD_{50} dose of tetra dioxin in male guinea pigs is 0.5–1.0 μg/kg, and in male and female rats, 22.5 and 45 μg/kg, respectively. Feeding *chicken edema factor* diets, containing dioxins, produced cumulative toxicity in monkeys.[9] Storage of hexa, hepta and octa isomers, as identified by GLC, has been reported in chickens and rats fed *chicken edema factor* diets.[10] Chronic administration of 2,4,5-T or 2,4-D to dogs produces cumulative toxicity with gastro-intestinal haemorrhage, suggestive of cumulative dioxin effects.[11]

G. Teratogenicity of Dioxins

1. FDA Studies (*FDA Conference, 2/24/70*)

A mixture of dioxins, 21% trichloro and 53% tetrachloro isomers, were injected in hamsters between days 6–10 of pregnancy over a dose range from 0.5 to 9.1 μg/kg/day. At the

---

[8] L. C. Silverstein, Dow Chemical Co. Memo. February 7, 1970. Safe Handling of Tetrachlorodibenzo-p-dioxin (TCBD) in the Laboratory.

[9] Allen, J. R. and Carstein, L. A. Light and electron microscopic observation in *Macaca mulatta* monkeys fed toxic fat.

[10] FDA. Unpublished data.

[11] Drill, V. A. and Hiratzka, T. *Ind. Hygiene & Occupat. Med.* I, 61–67, 1953.

highest dose, the incidence of fetal mortality was 82% and the incidence of congenital abnormalities, 82%. At the 0.5 μg/kg dose, there was a 5% incidence of abnormalities.

2. Dow Studies[12] (*Society of Toxicology meetings 3/17/70*)

The tetra dioxin isomer was fed to Sprague-Dawley rats between days 6–15 of pregnancy, over a dose range from 0.03 to 8.0 μg/kg/day. There was a marked increase in resorption sites at the 2μg level. Gastro-intestinal hemorrhages occurred over a range from 0.125 to 8 μg, dose-dependently. Additionally, at the 0.125 μg/kg level there was a decrease in male fetal weights.

It should be emphasized that cystic kidneys were not seen at the 0.125 μg/kg dose of the tetra isomer or even higher levels. In the Bionetics study, 2,4,5-T at 4.6 mg/kg, containing 25 ppm of the tetra dioxin isomer equivalent to 0.124 μg/kg, produced a 39% incidence of congenital abnormalities with cystic kidneys. There is thus a clear discrepancy between the teratogenic effects of 2,4,5-T containing 25 *ppm* of dioxin, and the effects of the equivalent concentration of the same dioxin. It is, however, conceivable that this discrepancy may reflect synergistic interactions between dioxin and 2,4,5-T.

H. Some Unresolved Problems

1. Chemical Composition of 2,4,5-T Formulations

Currently used 2,4,5-T formulations contain about 5% of known impurities, largely polychlorophenols. Analytic data on a sample of 2,4,5-T (Dow data, on production batch 120449) are as follows:

---

[12] Sparschu, G. L., Dunn, F. L., and Rowe, V. K. (Dow Chemical Co.) Teratogenic study of 2,3,7,8-Tetrachlorodibenzo-p-dioxin in the rat. Society of Toxicology 9th Annual Meeting. Atlanta, Georgia 3/17/70.

Composition of a 2,4,5-T Formulation	Percent
2,3,7,8-tetrachlorodibenzo-p-dioxin	(0.5 *ppm*)
2,6-dichlorophenoxyacetic acid	<0.02
2,5-dichlorophenoxyacetic acid	0.42
2,4-dichlorophenoxyacetic acid	0.05
2,3,6-trichlorophenoxyacetic acid	0.55
2,4,6-trichlorophenoxyacetic acid	<0.1
Bis- (2,4,5-trichlorophenoxy) acetic acid	0.4
3 isomers of dichloromethoxy phenoxyacetic acid	2.9
2,4,5-trichlorophenol	0.23 (max.)
sodium chloride	0.035
2,4,5-trichlorophenoxyacetic acid	Balance

There are no available data on the presence and concentration of the more than 60 positional isomers of dioxin, other than the 2,3,7,8-tetrachloro dioxin isomer, in this batch of 2,4,5-T, or in other batches produced for food crop or other purposes in the U.S., and abroad. In view of the relatively high concentration of polychlorophenol impurities in 2,4,5-T, it is likely that a wide range of dioxins are also present. 2,4-D and other phenoxy herbicides are similarly chemically uncharacterized. The higher positional dioxin isomers, hexa, hepta and octa, have been identified in 2,4-dichlorophenol, a precursor of 2,4-D. Apart from the presence of dioxins in polychlorophenols, heating of polychlorophenols will produce additional high yields of dioxin. Illustratively, heating 5 g of pentachlorophenol at 300°C for 12 hours yielded 1.5 g of the octa-dioxin isomer.[13] There are no available data on the possible production of dioxins from combustion of 2,4,5-T or 2,4-D. While improved production techniques may well reduce the levels of polychlorophenols and the levels of the 2,3,7,8-dioxin isomer, apart from other isomers, in 2,4,5-T and other phenoxy herbicides, the degree to which this is practical does not yet appear to have been clearly defined.

[13] Cowan, J. C. USDA Memo 2/12/70. Possible sources of polychlorodibenzodioxins in fats.

2.   Stability and Persistence of Dioxins

The extent of usage of 2,4,5-T and other phenoxy herbicides on food crops and for other purposes in the U.S. and abroad dictates the scale of resulting environmental contamination with 2,3,7,8-dioxin and other isomers. The following data are illustrative:

PRODUCTION AND USAGE ON CROPS OF PHENOXY HERBICIDES IN 1964 IN THE U.S.[14]

Phenoxy Herbicides	Production (lbs)	Use (lbs) on crops in 48 states, 1964
2,4-D	54,366,000	29,687,000 (ie, 63% of total production)
2,4,5-T	12,963,000	979,000 (ie, 13% of total production)
MCPA (Methylchloro-phenoxyacetic acid)		1,454,000
Other		684,000
		32,804,000

These data reflect deliberate applications of phenoxy herbicides to crops, and do not reflect unintentional crop contamination following the more extensive application of herbicides for brush control or other purposes. There are no available data on the extent of such unintentional contamination. It is, however, well known that phenoxy herbicide dusts may drift for miles, even on non-windy days, following routine application.[15] The concentration of phenoxy herbicides in the air in Washington in 1964[16] reached a maximum of 3.4 $\mu g/m^3$, with an average

---

[14] *Quantities of Pesticides Used by Farmers in 1964.* Agricultural Economic Report No. 131. Economic Research Service, USDA, Washington, D.C. 1968.

[15] Federal Register, May 21, 1969.

[16]Bamesberger, W. L., and Adams, D. R. In *Organic Pesticides in the Environment Advan. Chem. Ser. 60,* (1966).

of 0.045 $\mu g/m^3$. These figures probably underestimate the proportional concentration of atmospheric dioxins, in view of their high stability relative to phenoxy herbicides.

CALCULATED DIOXIN CONTAMINATION PER ACRE
FOLLOWING 2,4,5-T APPLICATION

Application 2,4,5-T (lbs/acre)	*Contamination with 2,3,7,8-Dioxin* (mg/acre)	
	Based on 0.5 ppm *Dioxin*	*Based on 25* ppm *Dioxin*
2.5 (domestic use)	0.57	2.8
25.0 (export use)	5.70	28.4

These calculations are based on the 2,3,7,8-dioxin alone, and ignore additional contamination due to other dioxin isomers. The figures for export use should be adjusted to reflect varying concentration of 2,4,5-T in different formulations.

The high concentration of polychlorophenolic impurities in 2,4,5-T, approximately 5%, apart from other sources of polychlorophenols, may result in extremely high yields of dioxins. As mentioned previously, heating of 5 g of pentachlorophenol at 300°C for 12 hours results in a yield of 1.5 g of the octadioxin isomer. Combustion of shrub, brush, timber, or other materials exposed to phenoxy herbicides or other polychlorophenols, may thus liberate high concentrations of dioxins in the atmosphere.

It is thus of interest to examine the data on stability and persistence of dioxins in the environment. The 2,3,7,8-tetra isomer is known to be heat stable up to 800°C. There are, however, no available data on the heat stability of other dioxin isomers. There are also no available data on the stability and persistence of the 2,3,7,8- and other dioxin isomers in soil, water, crops, milk, and animal or human tissues. Most importantly, there are no available data on the possible accumulation and transmission of 2,3,7,8- and other dioxins in the food chain—air, soil and water → plants, brush and crops → fish, birds and cattle → man, with attendant accumulation in man. The heat stability of the tetra isomer, the general lipid solubility of the dioxins, and their cumulative toxicity in experimental animals, all serve to enhance the possibility of food chain transmission of the various dioxin isomers.

3. Teratogenicity of Relatively Pure 2,4,5-T

The relatively contaminated 2,4,5-T used in the Bionetics study, containing about 27 *ppm* of the tetra-dioxin contaminant, induced congenital abnormalities in mice and rats, particularly cystic kidneys, that were not produced by the pure tetra dioxin. Illustratively, the contaminated 2,4,5-T at 4.6 mg/kg/day oral dose level in rats produced a 39% incidence of congenital abnormalities. This dose of 2,4,5-T is equivalent to 0.124 μg/kg/day of the tetra dioxin. However, as reported in the Dow studies (Society of Toxicology, Atlanta, 3/17/70), 0.125 μg/kg/day of the tetra dioxin did not produce cystic kidneys in rats. This discrepancy may however conceivably reflect synergistic interactions between 2,4,5-T and dioxins. Additionally, as indicated above, relatively pure 2,4,5-T, containing < 1 *ppm* of the tetra-dioxin contaminant, was teratogenic in preliminary studies with 3 species—mice, rats, and hamsters, over a dose range of 24–150 mg/kg. In some of these studies, *eg.,* in hamsters at 24 mg/kg/day, *no effect levels* were not reached.

Thus, recent studies on relatively pure 2,4,5-T clearly confirm its teratogenecity and lend further emphasis to the following conclusions of the report of the HEW teratogenicity panel:

> *The use of currently registered pesticides to which humans are exposed and which are found to be teratogenic by suitable test procedures in one or more mammalian species should be immediately restricted to prevent risk of human exposure.*

All these considerations confirm the following conclusion stated in the Bionetics report:

These results imply a hazard of teratogenesis in the use of this compound (2,4,5-T). The problems of extrapolation preclude definition of the hazard—but its existence seems clear.

4. Toxicology of Dioxins

The toxicology of dioxins is of particular interest in view of the previously reviewed data on the very high acute toxicity, embryotoxicity, cumulative chronic toxicity of 2,3,7,8 dioxin and related isomers, and also the stability, widespread environmental distribution, and likelihood of accumulation and transmission of any dioxins in the food chain.

There are no data in the available literature on the carcinogenicity or mutagenicity of positional isomers of dioxins. Recent studies on the teratogenicity of dioxins have been largely restricted to the 2,3,7,8 isomer; there are no available teratogenicity data on most of the other ·positional isomers. There are no available experimental data on behavioral or psychopharmacological effects due to dioxins; this would be of interest in view of the possible psychiatric effects described in humans exposed to dioxins. There are no data in the available literature on *any* toxicological studies on any dioxin isomer following acute or chronic administration by inhalation.

The extreme inadequacy of toxicological data on dioxins clearly precludes consideration of potential human hazards due to dioxins in air, food or water, and consideration of possible safety margins following exposure to dioxins.

I. Conclusions

I would like to re-emphasize the conclusions of the HEW panel on teratogenicity;

The use of currently registered pesticides to which humans are exposed and which are found to be teratogenic by suitable test procedures in one or more mammalian species should be immediately restricted to prevent risk of human exposure. Such pesticides, in current use, include Captan; Carbaryl; the butyl, isopropyl, and isooctyl esters of 2,4-D Folpet; mercurials; PCNB; and 2,4,5-T. The teratogenicity of 2,4-D, the other salts and esters of both 2,4-D and 2,4,5-T, and that of IPC should be investigated further.

Finally and critically, available data on the toxicology of the dioxins, and more importantly *the lack of data* on the toxicology—acute and chronic toxicity, carcinogenesis, mutagenesis, and teratogenesis—of the numerous positional isomers of dioxins, indicate an urgent need for restriction of human exposure to dioxins. Similar restrictions should extend to polychlorophenols, polychlorophenolic containing formulations, and their combustion products.

STATEMENT OF
JESSE L. STEINFELD, M.D.
SURGEON GENERAL, U.S. PUBLIC
HEALTH SERVICE, AND DEPUTY
ASSISTANT SECRETARY FOR HEALTH
& SCIENTIFIC AFFAIRS OF THE
DEPARTMENT OF HEALTH,
EDUCATION, AND WELFARE
BEFORE THE HART SUBCOMMITTEE

April 15, 1970

I am pleased to appear before you today to discuss the herbicide known as 2,4,5-T, our efforts to determine its hazard to health, and subsequent action to protect human health.

The production of 2,4,5-T (2,4,5-trichlorophenoxyacetic acid) in the United States increased from eight to 40 million pounds per year in the last decade. In the U.S., 2,4,5 -T is principally used as a weed-killer in clearing range and pasturelands, roadsides and rights-of-way, in suppressing aquatic weeds, and in eliminating weeds in crop lands. It is also used to reduce weeds in turf. The use of 2,4,5-T and its salts and esters on food crops has been registered by the U.S. Department of Agriculture on the basis of "no residues" in the marketed food. To insure that the foods reaching markets are free of residues, the FDA has monitored the food supply in selected cities. About 5300 food samples were analyzed for 2,4,5-T and other pesticides in the last 4 years. Residues of 2,4,5-T, at trace levels (less than 0.1 part per million) were found in 25 of these samples. In 1965, one sample contained 0.19 parts per million; in 1966, another sample contained 0.29 parts per million. It is my opinion that the results of the monitoring program justified the registered use of 2,4,5-T on selected food crops, in the absence of any known toxicity of 2,4,5-T.

The development of a balanced public policy which considers benefits and risks associated with the use of a compound such as 2,4,5-T is an exceptionally difficult matter. Great public fear of the possible implications for man has followed reports of harm in laboratory animal tests. And yet frequently it is not known with certainty what laboratory animal tests may mean for man. We are obligated to make decisions of great health and economic importance on the basis of very limited evidence of potential hazard; prudence allows no other course. We are aware that both good and bad consequences may result from our actions.

The enormous strides taken in achieving the prosperous and healthy life we now enjoy in an industrial age has created problems and uncertainties which are not easily overcome. The resolution of these uncertainties and solution of these problems will require national commitment and broad public education and understanding.

At this point, I would now like to read the joint announcement of Secretaries Hardin, Finch and Hickel, prepared in accord with the Interagency Agreement for Protection of the Public Health and the Quality of the Environment in Relation to Pesticides.

"Agriculture Secretary Clifford M. Hardin, Interior Secretary Walter J. Hickel, and HEW Secretary Robert H. Finch today announced the immediate suspension by Agriculture of the registrations of liquid formulations of the weed killer, 2,4,5-T for use around the home and for registered uses on lakes, ponds, and ditch banks.

"These actions are being taken pursuant to the Interagency Agreement for Protection of the Public Health and the Quality of the Environment in Relation to Pesticides among the three Departments.

"The three Cabinet Officers also announced that the Department of Agriculture intends to *cancel registered uses of non-liquid formulations of 2,4,5-T around the home and on all food crops for human consumption (apples, blueberries, barley, corn, oats, rye, rice and sugar cane) for which it is presently registered.*

"The suspension actions were based on the opinion of the Department of Health, Education, and Welfare that contamination resulting from uses of 2,4,5-T around the home and in water areas could constitute a hazard to human health.

"New information reported to HEW on Monday, April 13, 1970, indicates that 2,4,5-T, as well as its contaminant dioxins, may produce abnormal development in unborn animals. Nearly pure 2,4,5-T was reported to cause birth defects when injected at high doses into experimental pregnant mice, but not in rats. No data on humans are available.

"These actions *do not eliminate registered use of 2,4,5-T for control of weeds and brush on range, pasture, forest, rights of way and other non-agricultural land.* Users are cautioned that 2,4,5-T should not be used near homes or recreation areas. Registered uses are being reviewed by the three Departments to make certain that they include adequate precautions against grazing treated areas long enough after treatment by 2,4,5-T so that no contaminated meat or milk results from animals grazing the treated area.

"While residues of 2,4,5-T in meat and milk are very rare, such residues are illegal and render contaminated products subject to seizure. There is no tolerance for 2,4,5-T on meat, milk or any other feed or food.

"USDA will issue guidelines for disposal of household products containing 2,4,5-T. The *chemical is biologically decomposed* in a moist environment.

Background Information

"Secretary Finch's Commission on Pesticides, which reported its findings in November and December 1969, expressed concern that research conducted at Bionetics Research Laboratories, under the direction of the National Cancer Institute, indicated that 2,4,5-T had produced a number of birth defects when fed or injected into certain strains of mice and rats. Because the test material contained substantial concentrations of chemical impurities (dioxins), the birth abnormalities could not be attributed with certainty either to 2,4,5-T, or to the impurities known to be present.

"Representatives of the chemical industry pointed to evidence of extreme potency of the impurities as toxic agents. They demonstrated that 2,4,5-T now being marketed is of a greater purity than that which had been tested in the Bionetics experiments and urged that further testing be undertaken to clarify the questions raised.

"Responding to this suggestion and utilizing materials supplied by one of the major producers of 2,4,5-T, scientists at the National Institute of Environmental Health Sciences promptly initiated studies to determine whether 2,4,5-T itself, its impurities or a combination of both had caused the earlier findings, and whether the 2,4,5-T now being marketed produces birth abnormalities in mice and rats.

"The experiments were completed last week and the statistical analyses performed over the weekend. On Monday and Tuesday of this week the analyses of the data were presented to the regulatory agencies of the Federal Government and to the members of the Cabinet.

"The dioxin impurities and the 2,4,5-T as it is now manufactured, separately produced birth abnormalities in the experimental mice.

"Because absolutely pure 2,4,5-T was not available for testing, it is possible only to infer from certain of the observations that the pure 2,4,5-T probably would be found to be teratogenic if it were tested. But, since pure 2,4,5-T is not marketed and could not be produced in commercial quantities, this is not a practical issue for consideration.

"In exercising its responsibility to safeguard public health and safety, the regulatory agencies of the Federal Government will move immediately to minimize human exposure to 2,4,5-T and its impurities. The measures being taken are designed to provide maximum protection to women in the childbearing years by eliminating formulation of 2,4,5-T use in household, aquatic and recreational areas. Its use on food crops will be cancelled, and its use on range and pastureland will be controlled. Maximum surveillance of water supplies and marketed foods will be maintained as a measure of the effectiveness of these controls. These measures will be announced more specifically in the Federal Register shortly.

"While the restriction to be imposed upon the use of this herbicide may cause some economic hardship, we must all cooperate to protect human health from potential hazards of 2,4,5-T, other pesticides and the dioxins.

"The three Secretaries commended the chemical industry for its prompt and willing cooperation with the National Institute of Environmental Health Sciences in the studies to clarify questions raised by the initial studies of this herbicide and for working closely with the FDA in the other studies still underway. They urged the full support of industry, agriculture and the home gardener in insuring the safe use of 2,4,5-T and other pesticides which contribute in important ways to the welfare of the Nation."

At this point, we would like to provide for the record a summary description of the results of these latest studies of the National Institute of Environmental Health Sciences, completed this past week. I shall be pleased to respond to questions about these data but suggest that the Committee not be burdened by a detailed oral presentation of the findings which have been stated briefly in the foregoing announcement.

This leads me to brief mention of the studies which will be presented next by Dr. Verrett. Commencing in the Fall of 1969, Dr. Verrett re-instituted tests of the embryo-toxicity and teratogenicity of 2,4,5-T, its contaminating dioxins and related chemicals. Dr. Verrett is to be commended for promptly attacking these problems and for going to the very considerable trouble of purifying the 2,4,5-T by repeated re-crystallization. However, I must express concern about the degree of reliance which can be placed upon chick embryo studies. While the studies in chick embryos are in *general* agreement with those in rodents studied at the NIEHS, it is to be emphasized that they do not clarify the uncertainties as to significance for man.

I believe that it is imperative that everyone involved in the development of a national policy for dealing with the many questions posed by 2,4,5-T and other pesticides be aware of the complexity as well as the importance of the issues, together with the limitations of our ability to estimate potential hazards to human health posed by these substances. It is essential that we strive to respond wisely to the discoveries which have been made in this field, and resist the temptation to resort to measures which may be more extreme than the evidence warrants. For example, 2,4,5-T is probably the most effective means of controlling poison ivy, poison oak, and other noxious weeds to which a substantial portion of the population react badly. It has been estimated that 60% of the American population is sensitive to either poison ivy or poison oak, and that from 5–10% of Americans suffer a reaction to the poisons from these weeds each year. Some of these individuals become quite ill and incapacitated by their reaction to these poisons. By contrast, we are not aware of any reliable evidence that 2,4,5-T, indeed any of the pesticidal chemicals, has resulted in human birth abnormalities. These remarks should not be interpreted as evidence of indifference to what may be a potential hazard to health. The record clearly reveals a series of responsible actions by the Administration to the results of recent laboratory tests. Prudence has characterized the decisions and actions and will continue to guide the Department in these matters.

In keeping with the pattern established with the naming of the Secretary's Commission on Pesticides, the thorough study of pesticide problems by the Commission, and the Administration's prompt action to implement the recommendations of the Commission, we now commit ourselves to the following actions:

We shall strive to develop better means for predicting in laboratory animal systems the potential hazard posed for man by chemical pesticides.

We are aware of a great need for a centralized clearinghouse for information of all types on pesticides. We plan to have such a clearinghouse established jointly by the National Library of Medicine and the FDA in the very near future. Other agencies having similar interests and needs will be invited to participate in this undertaking.

The need to continue certain closely restricted uses of 2,4,5-T will require a high level of surveillance activity to insure protection of the human population from exposure through water sources. This will be done.

The Food and Drug Administration will continue to examine a variety of foods for the possible presence of residues of pesticides, and will take appropriate action through the Interdepartmental Agreement to protect the public health.

STATEMENT BY
M. JACQUELINE VERRETT, Ph.D.
DIVISION OF TOXICOLOGY
FOOD AND DRUG ADMINISTRATION
U.S. DEPARTMENT OF HEALTH,
EDUCATION, AND WELFARE
BEFORE THE HART SUBCOMMITTEE

April 15, 1970

Thank you, Mr. Chairman, for this opportunity to discuss our investigations of the relationships between chlorinated phenoxy herbicides, chlorinated dibenzo-p-dioxins, and the chick edema factors.

Chick edema disease was first recognized in 1957, when large numbers of broiler flocks in the United States suffered what appeared to be an epidemic disease. The affected birds appeared droopy, with ruffled feathers, and had difficulty breathing. In many flocks, more than 50% of the birds died as a result of the disease. Of the millions of birds affected, those autopsied consistently displayed hydropericardium (accumulation of fluid in the pericardial sac), accumulation of fluid in the abdominal cavity, subcutaneous edema, and additionally liver and kidney damage. In 1958 the investigations of a number of laboratories indicated that the causal agent was contained in fats, and specifically in the unsaponifiable fraction of fats in the commercial poultry rations. In laying hens the toxic fat caused a rapid drop in egg production. Pullets receiving toxic fat during the full growing period did not come into production, and mortality was very high. Hydropericardium, the most common lesion found in young birds, was not found in birds of laying age.

The chick edema factors found in the toxic fat in the 1957

outbreak was presumed to have arisen as a by-product of industrial production of stearic and oleic acids, since the unsaponifiable materials from this process were components of fat in the poultry ration. Subsequently, the toxic substance was found to be present in several different types of fats. It was demonstrated to be present in samples of commercially produced oleic acids and triolein, in acidulated vegetable oils, and in inedible animal tallows. The demonstration of the presence of the chick edema factor in commercial fats led to the ruling by the Food and Drug Administration in 1961 that higher fatty acids intended for food additive use must be free of the chick edema factors. The presence of the factor was to be ascertained by a chick bioassay based on the volume of pericardial fluid in birds fed the fat under investigation.

Beginning in 1958 fat that had first been proved to be toxic to chicks was used by various investigators in experiments with other species, and was demonstrated also to produce deleterious effects in rats, mice, turkeys, pigeons, guinea pigs, swine, dogs, and monkeys.

Early investigations of feeding toxic fats to rats indicated that they are more resistant than chicks in short-term feedings, but when fed in sufficient dosage, extracts of the toxic fat produced definite deleterious effects as shown by growth depression, enlarged and fatty livers, marked involution of the thymus, and enlarged adrenals.

Guinea pigs fed 2½% toxic fat stopped growing at six weeks, and death losses occurred at eight weeks. At a level of 4½% the weight losses occurred after three weeks, and death at four weeks. The pathology observed was congestion of the lungs and mottled livers.

Dogs fed 10% toxic fat in their rations lost hair on their backs and shoulders (alopecia), and there was poor reproduction and lactation performance. Whelped pups were either dead or weak, and the mothers seemed to have an insufficient milk supply. Pups removed before weaning and fed a normal ration showed an immediate and dramatic increase in growth. Other litters maintained on the toxic fat ration post-weaning demonstrated inferior growth performance.

Monkeys have demonstrated considerable sensitivity to toxic fat materials. In one study nine monkeys received a toxic triolein at a level of 25% in their diets. One monkey died at one month, and four died at three months. At the three month period, corn oil was substituted for the toxic triolein, but the other four monkeys died from three weeks to five months later, in spite of this substitution. Of the nine monkeys fed the toxic triolein, eight were autopsied and showed signs of jaundice, pancreatic atrophy and fibrosis, hemosiderosis, fatty liver with necrosis, bile duct proliferation, and gross hemorrhage in the intestinal tract. No such pathology was seen in the control monkeys in this study.

A second study with thirty-six monkeys given a toxic fat at levels from 0.125 to 10% of their diet, demonstrated an inverse relationship between the concentration of the toxic fat in the diet and their mean survival time. Those given the highest level (10%) had a mean survival time of only 91 days, while those given the lowest level (0.125%) had a mean survival time of 445 days. It has been estimated that the highest level provided approximately 728 μg total chick edema factors, while the lowest level diet provided approximately 100 μg total intake. The toxic fat was lethal *at all* levels studied, and the animals were sacrificed when possible just before death. During the last 30 days of life, all monkeys developed alopecia, generalized subcutaneous edema, accumulation of fluid in the abdominal and thoracic cavities, and hydropericardium. There were decreases in red and white blood cell counts, total serum protein values, and altered serum-protein ratios. There was also cardiac dilatation and myocardial hypertrophy and edema. Finally, the experimental monkeys had reduced hematopoiesis and spermatogenesis, degeneration of the blood vessels, focal necrosis of the liver and gastric ulcers.

Limited experimentation with mice, pigeons, and turkeys, indicated that toxic fat in the diet led to reduction in growth without hydropericardium or accumulation of abdominal fluid. Similarly, swine, fed toxic fat at a level of 9% of their ration, showed poor weight gain, but one pig sacrificed six weeks after the start of the study showed no gross or microscopic lesions attributable to the ration.

One important finding in the studies with chickens, is the apparent storage of the chick edema factors in chick tissues. The unsaponifiable fraction of carcasses (exclusive of intestines, head, and feet) of chickens fed the toxic fat was very potent in producing hydropericardium in other birds when incorporated in their rations. Other investigations of the distribution of the chick edema factors in the chick tissues indicated significant levels in bone, heart, intestine, kidney, liver, and skin. The liver contained more than 80% of the total detected. A similar determination of the distribution in rats indicated the presence of chick edema factors only in liver and in the feces.

During the years that the previously described toxicity investigations were taking place, the toxic fats were undergoing intensive chemical analyses to concentrate, purify, and finally determine the nature of the compounds responsible for chick edema disease. At all steps of these procedures, the path of the toxic material was confirmed by assay in young chicks. This proved to be a time-consuming and difficult job because of the complexity of the fatty materials. A major breakthrough in this effort came when it was found that a highly purified crystalline material possessing the properties of chick edema factor contained chlorine. This indicated that it was not a natural component of the fat in which it occurred.

Work in several laboratories obtained similar results, and examination of the purified material by a variety of analytical techniques suggested that chick edema factors could be highly substituted (chlorinated) derivatives of naphthalene, biphenyl, anthracene, or even structures common to the chlorinated pesticides of the DDT family. These latter compounds were ruled out when tested in the chick feeding assay, but some derivatives of the former classes of compounds were tested and found in some instances to be toxic, and indeed produce similar lesions to those observed with authentic toxic fat. However, none of these compounds demonstrated the high order of toxicity, or the complete chick edema syndrome when so tested. Finally, by means of single crystal x-ray crystallography, it was demonstrated that a pure compound isolated from a toxic fat was a hexachloro-dibenzo-p-dioxin. This structure was verified by infra-red, ultra-violet, and mass spectrometry data. Final confirmation came when this particular compound was synthesized and found to produce the same lesions in chicks as the compound isolated from the toxic fat.

The finding that a chlorinated dibenzo-p-dioxin was a chick edema factor explained why different investigators had isolated materials similar in their capacity to elicit chick edema disease, but yet in their purest forms, had slightly different chemical properties. The large number of isomers possible (more than 60) in this family ranging from mono- to octa-chloro-dibenzo-p-dioxins illustrates the complexity of the problem. It then became a problem of determining whether some or all of these compounds are in fact chick edema factors, and what their relative capacities in this regard might be.

The chlorinated dibenzo-p-dioxin structures have been known in organic chemistry many years, and became particularly noteworthy, when in manufacturing processes with chlorophenols, their formation as by-products posed serious occupational hazards. The most potent in this regard seems to have been the symmetrical tetrachloro-p-dioxin which was formed in the manufacture of 2,4,5-trichlorophenol. These chlorinated compounds were found to cause a serious and persistent disease referred to as chloracne. This disease was first described in 1899. Associations of this disease with chlorinated dibenzo-p-dioxins were made by the Germans, who had several outbreaks of this disease in their factories. There have also been similar occurrences in the Netherlands and in this country, in factories manufacturing chlorophenol compounds. It should also be pointed out, that other compounds, such as the chlorinated naphthalenes, anthracenes, biphenyls and dibenzofurans, are known to be acnegenic, but as in the case of the toxic response in chicks, these materials are less potent than the chlorinated dibenzo-p-dioxins. In the case of the chloracne associated with dioxin, the human symptomatology extends to other mucous membrane irritation, porphyria cutanea tarda, hirsutism, hyperpigmentation, increased skin fragility, severe damage to the internal organs, particularly hepatotoxicity, and central nervous system disorders, as indicated by neuromuscular symptoms and psychologic alterations, and other systemic symptoms. Most of these occupational exposures in Germany occurred in the 1950's, and follow-up examination of these affected workers in recent years indicate that the recovery period is lengthy, with many workers still having demonstrable adverse effects from prior exposure. Similar observations have been made on exposed workers in the U.S.A. The tetrachlorodibenzo-p-dioxin was demonstrated to produce the chloracne in humans after the application of only 20 micrograms. The rabbit ear is especially sensitive, with concentrations of 0.001 to 0.005% producing severe reactions after local application. This assay using the rabbit ear is apparently used as an indicator in some plants of the content of this particular dioxin in the manufacturing process. Hence, the serious health significance of these compounds for humans has, inadvertently, been clearly documented.

Research in Germany and Japan indicated that the magnitude of this problem was indeed large, since the formation of the chlorinated di-benzo-p-dioxins would be facilitated in the saponification procedures used in various processes involving chlorophenols. A further complication is that a given chlorophenol preparation is generally contaminated with other isomers, increasing the possibility of formation of a wide spectrum of chlorinated di-benzo-p-dioxins beyond those to be expected from the predominant component. Evidence that this does occur will be discussed shortly in connection with the chicken embryo studies of these materials.

During the time the previously described investigations of

the chick edema factors were underway, many of which were carried out by F.D.A. investigators, methodology was developed for detecting the chick edema factors using sensitive gas-liquid-chromatographic (GLC) techniques. It became apparent that authentic toxic fats consistently gave peaks with specific retention times, and these peaks were used as an indication of chick edema factor in a suspect sample. Confirmation of this was obtained using the chick feeding assay. In the light of recent knowledge of the chlorodioxins as chick edema factors, it has been possible to establish that the materials being detected were hexa-, hepta-, and octa-chlorodibenzo-p-dioxins. Although toxic fat samples did indeed contain peaks corresponding to dioxins of lesser chlorine content, i.e. di-, tri-, tetra-, penta-, these are not detectable with this particular analytical procedure because their particular peaks are obscured by other components, including pesticide residues present in the samples. Other GLC procedures are being developed to detect these latter dioxins.

In the early 1960's the chicken embryo was being used in toxicological evaluations of a wide variety of materials. It was hoped to develop a rapid and sensitive screening system to pinpoint compounds with significant toxic and teratogenic effects for further study. In view of the demonstrated sensitivity of the chicken to chick edema factors, the chicken embryo was used to assay toxic fat samples, and found to present the same syndrome as observed in the chick feeding assay. A high mortality was observed with toxic fat extracts, and additionally, hydropericardium, generalized and massive edema, eye, beak, and leg defects, and necrotic livers were apparent on gross observation. No microscopic studies have been conducted on embryos or hatched chicks in these investigations.

In parallel with other investigations, the chicken embryo was used to test the toxicity of the chick edema factors isolated from toxic fats. It was also found that the chlorinated biphenyls, naphthalenes, anthracenes, and other compounds did indeed elicit a toxic response, and in some instances, the chick edema syndrome was present. But in no case were any of these materials as potent as the toxic components isolated from toxic fats, and were generally less potent by a few orders of magnitude.

After the identification in 1966 of a hexachloro dibenzo-p-dioxin as a chick edema factor, studies were initiated in which various isomers of chlorinated dibenzo-p-dioxin were prepared and tested in the embryos. Although the investigation was not extensive or complete, it illustrated that isomers prepared by pyrolyzing selected chlorophenols did give chloro-dibenzo-p-dioxins with GLC retention times duplicating those in the authentic toxic fats, and likewise, produced the chick edema syndrome in the treated embryos. It was also apparent from this study that the various isomers (that is, those with different chlorine content, and those with identical chlorine content, but with chlorine atoms positioned differently on the molecule) varied in their toxicity, although in all cases only microgram or less quantities were required to elicit the toxic response. It is not possible to give exact figures for the toxicities obtained in this study, since most of the individual dioxins were contaminated with traces of others. Nevertheless, it was apparent that the symmetrical chloro-dioxin prepared from 2,4,5-trichlorophenol (2,3,6,7-tetrachloro dibenzo-p-dioxin) was more potent than any of the others tested, even recognizing its lack of purity.

During this investigation, samples of the chlorophenols, both technical and reagent grades, were examined by GLC to determine if pre-formed chloro-dioxins were present. The presence of chloro-dioxins was demonstrated by GLC, and these materials, which can be removed by appropriate techniques, were then tested in the chicken embryo system and did indeed produce chick edema. A current study of similarly contaminated chlorophenols, containing from 18 ppm to 95 ppm of chloro-dioxins with six or more chlorine atoms are currently under test.

This investigation was not pursued further in view of the

fact that there had been no known occurrences of chick edema disease since the late 1950's, and hence, such research had a low order of priority. However, in early 1969, there was another large outbreak of the disease in North Carolina, and the toxic factor was traced to the fat component of the feed. The toxicity was confirmed by the chicken embryo test with fractions of the hexa-, hepta-, and octa-chlorodibenzo-p-dioxins from the crude fat. An investigation of the processing plant in which the toxic vegetable oil products were produced revealed a proximate operation for the manufacture of chlorophenol formulations. However, it is still not possible to conclude that this accounted solely for the presence of dioxins in the fat, or whether they were at least to some extent present in crude oil from a prior contamination. Since that time, F.D.A. has initiated an investigation of the oils of other manufacturers and processors, and in a few cases GLC analysis has indicated the presence of chloro-dioxins. These have not as yet been confirmed by chicken embryo bioassay; however, it is noteworthy that in the case of these suspect samples, there is no known adjacent manufacturing operation that would give rise to direct chloro-dioxin or chlorophenol contamination, so that entry of the chloro-dioxins from others sources must be considered.

This 1969 outbreak of chick edema disease, coupled with the question of contamination of the herbicide 2,4,5-T by chlorinated dioxins led us to renew this investigation. In the past six months the herbicides 2,4-D and 2,4,5-T, as well as the particular tetrachlorodioxin purported to be the teratogenic agent responsible for the effects in the Bionetics study of 2,4,5-T have been under study. In an effort to assess the edema-producing capacity, the teratogenic activity, and the acute toxicity of these materials, samples of the original Bionetics 2,4,5-T (from Diamond-Alkali) were obtained for comparison with a sample representative of the current manufacture of Dow Chemical Co.

The Bionetics 2,4,5-T is reported to contain 27 ± 8 ppm of the 2,3,6,7-tetrachloro dibenzo-p-dioxin, with the content of other dioxins unknown. The current production of Dow 2,4,5-T has 0.5 ppm of this dioxin, with no analysis for higher chloro-dioxins reported, but does contain almost 5% of other impurities, mostly isomers of 2,4-D; 2,4,5-T; and chlorophenols and chlorophenoxy compounds of undetermined structure.

All investigations using the chicken embryo involved administration of the compounds by injection through the air cell of the egg, either pre-incubation or at the fourth day of incubation. A comparison of the Bionetics 2,4,5-T with the Dow 2,4,5-T indicates that with respect to the ability of the materials to produce embryonic mortality, the Bionetics 2,4,5-T is more potent. The Bionetics 2,4,5-T has an LD_{50} (that is, kills 50% of the treated embryos) of approximately $25\mu g$ per egg (0.5 ppm), while the Dow 2,4,5-T LD_{50} is approximately 100 μg per egg (2 ppm). With respect to teratogenic effects, both samples produce chick edema syndrome in the non-viable embryos, and hatched chicks, including eye defects, beak defects (predominantly cleft palate), short and twisted feet (the result of tendon slippage), and diffuse and localized edema in various parts of the body. With both of these samples of 2,4,5-T these teratogenic effects are observed at levels inducing no significant embryonic mortality. The Dow 2,4,5-T still produces the chick edema syndrome at 50 μg (1 ppm), a level where only 12% mortality is observed, while the Bionetics sample has similar effects as low as 6.25 μg per egg (0.125 ppm) a level inducing only 16% mortality. Both of these mortalities are close to that induced by the solvent alone. It should also be emphasized that the chick edema syndrome is not observed in the embryos treated with the solvents only, at any level, or in the control flock.

A sample of 2,4,5-T from a chemical supply company was subjected to three recrystallizations before test. With the present GLC techniques no choro-dioxins are detectable in this purified sample. When tested in embryos, it produced chick edema syndrome at 5, 10 and 25 ppm, all levels which induced no more than 15% mortality in the embryos. This same sample was subjected to an additional purification by seven extractions to remove dioxins that might have been present, but were below the current detection levels. This repurified sample is still clearly teratogenic in the embryos, since when tested at a level of 2.5 ppm it produced a 20% incidence of the malformations previously described, though no significant edema was seen grossly. The mortality induced was 24%, which is higher than that of the sample prior to the extensive extraction procedure. It is also noteworthy that the embryonic mortality occurred soon after treatment, and the hatched chicks had bleached down, indicative of an aberration in the normal pigment formation.

With respect to the 2,3,6,7-tetrachlorodibenzo-p-dioxin, early investigations of this compound in a preparation containing some 2,3,7-trichlorodibenzo-p-dioxin indicate a high order of toxicity and teratogenicity. Whether prepared by pyrolysis of 2,4,5-trichlorophenol, or direct chlorination of dibenzo-p-dioxin, the test preparations, which contained approximately 50–55% of the tetrachlorodioxin and 20–25% of the trichlorodioxin, produced significant mortality (that is greater than 20%) and chick edema syndrome in more than 40% of the treated embryos at levels of five ten-millionths of a milligram per egg, or 10 parts per trillion. More recent investigations, with two samples of the tetrachlorodioxin, both of purity greater than 95%, indicate edema and terata at 20 parts per trillion. These samples have only become available within the past month, and additional testing is underway at lower and higher levels.

It should also be mentioned that the herbicide 2,4-D as a commercially available sample, and a purified sample, a mixture of the N-butyl esters of 2,4-D and 2,4,5-T, and a sample of Silvex, a related herbicide have been tested. Terata and chick edema syndrome have been observed with all of these materials at levels of 10 ppm and above. Lower levels are under investigation, and the levels of dioxins in these samples are also being determined.

Studies have recently been initiated in the F.D.A. using pregnant golden hamsters, intubated on day 6 through 10 of organogenesis with the test compounds.

The Dow 2,4,5-T (0.5 ppm tetrachlorodioxin) tested at 100 mg/kg yielded about 80% fetal deaths and those pups born alive had gastrointestinal hemorrhages. The thrice-recrystallized 2,4,5-T sample referred to earlier, with no detectable chlorodioxins, when tested at a level of 100 mg/kg produced an average fetal mortality of 55%. Among 38 live pups, three abnormals were found, one with a deformed hind limb, and two with inadequate fusion of the skull. At lower doses the fetal mortality was less, but still higher than that observed in control hamsters. When the extensively repurified sample of 2,4,5-T was tested in hamsters no gross terata were observed at 100 mg/kg, but the number of early fetal deaths was 70% indicating a definite embryotoxic effect, and corroborating the observation of increased mortality in the chick embryo studies. Additional tests with this compound are underway.

A dioxin preparation containing approximately 51% 2,3,6,7-tetrachloro- and 21% 2,3,6-trichlorodibenzo-p-dioxin yielded 98% fetal deaths at 9.1 μg/kg. Gastrointestinal hemorrhages and eye anomalies (absence of lid) were present in many of the pups. Tests with the purer tetrachlorodibenzo-p-dioxins are underway. The numbers of animals in the hamster tests are too small to be considered statistically valid, but there are definite indications that alterations in fetal viability and gastrointestinal hemorrhages do occur at the levels tested.

In summary, the chick embryo studies, and additionally the preliminary hamster data, indicate that the current production 2,4,5-T containing 0.5 ppm of the 2,3,6,7-tetrachlorodibenzo-p-dioxin is teratogenic and embryotoxic in these test systems. Further, an extensively purified 2,4,5-T sample, with no chlorodioxins detectable with the present techniques has indicated significant embryotoxicity in the hamster and chick embryo, and additionally produced gross terata in the chicken embryos, making it impossible at this point in time to exonerate it of teratogenic or other adverse effects on the embryos that may have some health significance. The data for 2,4-D in chick embryos likewise demonstrate these effects in current production materials.

These studies have in no way assessed another, and perhaps more complicated, aspect of this problem, and that is the interactions of the various chlorodioxin isomers with each other in the many combinations in which they are likely to occur, or the possible interactions (including potentiation or synergism) between the chlorodioxins and the chlorophenols, herbicides, and other materials in which they are found.

STATEMENT OF
THE SURGEON GENERAL
BEFORE THE HART SUBCOMMITTEE

June 18, 1970

I am pleased to appear before you to discuss the actions that have been taken to protect the public health by the Department of Health, Education, and Welfare regarding the chlorophenoxyacid herbicides, particularly 2,4,5-T and 2,4-D.

During our last appearance before this Committee, we took note of certain needs to increase the Federal Government's effectiveness in dealing with questions of hazards to the public health presented by the pesticides, and pledge ourselves to action. We have made progress, even in the extremely short time since our April 15, 1970 announcement.

We are now defining how best to undertake to study the means for predicting, in laboratory animal systems, the potential hazards posed for man by chemical pesticides. It is certainly desirable, and may prove essential that we find some means of extrapolating the results from feeding animals very large doses of pesticide chemicals to the real life situation in which man is exposed for a long period to very minute amounts of these chemicals. However, I must emphasize that even with results based on studies in two species of mammals uncertainties remain as to the significance of those studies when applied to man: Complete information on the pesticides is essential to the efficient performance of all agencies concerned with the public health aspects of pesticides be they Federal, State or local. A centralized clearinghouse for information on all types of pesticides, is being established jointly by the National Library of Medicine and the Food and Drug Administration. The Division of Toxicology of FDA and the National Library of Medicine are now sharing toxicological information and are building on this base to form the clearinghouse. I am very pleased with the progress on this information center so far.

The Food and Drug Administration has issued instructions that special attention to the extent of available resources is to be given to the analysis for residues of 2,4,5-T on food crops for which this herbicide was formerly registered for use. This step was taken as an additional precaution to prevent accidental exposure to residues of 2,4,5-T even though our surveillance activities have not detected significant residues of 2,4,5-T on these food crops.

The scientific research on which the April 15, 1970 announcement was based was continued.

The National Institute of Environmental Health Sciences is conducting further research on 2,4,5-T, certain related herbicide compounds and 2,3,7,8 tetrachlorodibenzoparadioxin. Additional studies on the teratology of 2,4,5-T and tetrachloro dioxin in the random bred mouse have confirmed the earlier studies that 2,4,5-T produces cleft palate in the mouse. One study which utilized a combination of tetrachloro dioxin and the purest 2,4,5-T available indicates that there is no synergistic effect of these two compounds on the production of cleft palate.

Preliminary studies have been initiated with three esters of 2,4,5-T, namely the isobutyl ester, the isooctyl ester and the propylene glycol butyl ester. The experimental design is the same as that used to study 2,4,5-T. The results that are available to date are suggestive that at least some esters may be comparable in teratogenic activity to that of 2,4,5-T. At this time more definitive studies on these esters are underway. In addition, a teratogenic evaluation of Silvex, a compound structurally related to 2,4,5-T, will be initiated shortly. Also, another dioxin, the octochlorodibenzo-para-dioxin will be evaluated for its teratogenic potential.

Another line of research currently in progress is the delineation of the sequence of toxicologic processes which develop upon administration of tetrachlorodioxin to adult rats. The test parameters being evaluated are hematology, clinical chemistry, enzyme chemistry and histopathology. This study is still in progress but suggests major hepatic dysfunction as the primary toxicologic action of tetrachlorodioxin. In conjunction with this study, the octochlorodioxin will be studied for its toxicologic properties.

The Food and Drug Administration has launched a broad program of research to determine if herbicides such as 2,4,5-T and 2,4-D as they are now manufactured could pose a potential health hazard. The research on 2,4,5-T has led into a new area of investigation, in particular I refer here to the finding of the dioxin contamination in production batches of 2,4,5-T. This contamination has proven to be a series of chlorodibenzo-p-dioxin compounds containing various amounts and positional arrangements of chlorine atoms on the dioxin molecules. This contamination may arise through the unwanted synthesis of the dioxins during manufacture of 2,4,5-T from trichlorophenol, but the possibility exists that the dioxins are present in the chlorophenol material prior to its use in 2,4,5-T manufacture.

The chlorophenol class of chemicals themselves are widely used in our environment. Pentachlorophenol, for instance, is one of the most useful compounds available for the preservation of wood. Thus we find it prudent to and have extended investigations to include dioxin contamination of chlorophenols as well as to continue our investigations into the herbicides and the dioxins.

The FDA has a continuing project under way to examine various chlorophenol compounds containing from 1 to 5 chlorine atoms for the presence of dioxin contamination. Some chlorophenols have been tested at a concentration of 40 parts per million in the chick embryo and found to be toxic. The tentative, and I must emphasize tentative, results from these studies indicate that various dioxins may occur in chlorophenols. Mass spectrometry has identified dioxins in some of these chlorophenols. This work is being done in conjunction with the effort to improve the analytic chemistry necessary to detect the dioxin contamination in the herbicides.

At this time the chick embryo toxicity test is the most sensitive biological indication of the presence of dioxins, particularly tetrachlorodibenzo-p-dioxin. It is slow however, and more rapid methods of detecting dioxins must be established. The electron capture gas chromatographic method is now the most rapid and sensitive instrumental method available. In order to study the dioxins it has been necessary to produce dioxins of known purity and chlorine content. FDA now has produced a number of these. FDA is starting a study at the Perrine, Florida laboratory to determine the effect of various chlorophenols on mammalian systems using the golden hamster as the test animal. The golden hamster is worthy of note as a laboratory animal for this purpose. It is of a convenient size, easily housed, and has a gestation period of only 15 days giving a somewhat quicker test than the rat.

We are thus moving rapidly to develop adequate data from investigations designed to reveal any hazard to the public health from the use of the chlorophenoxy herbicides such as 2,4,5-T and 2,4-D or the chlorophenol compounds. The restrictive measures taken against 2,4,5-T, when in my judgment a hazard to the public health existed, are familiar to all of us. 2,4-D, another widely used herbicide chemical must be studied because of its uses on food crops. We must be certain that this compound does not constitute a health hazard.

At this writing, the FDA studies on 2,4,5-T in the golden hamster have served to confirm our earlier indications that 2,4,5-T per se could produce terata and embryotoxicity.

Samples of 2,4,5-T from two manufacturers, when given at 100 mg/kg to hamsters by gastric intubation (introducing the material directly into the stomach) produced an increased incidence of fetal mortality and one sample also produced terata. Neither of these samples contained any measurable symmetrical tetrachlorodibenzo-p-dioxin. Additional studies will be made to measure the dose-response relationship for teratogenicity of pure 2,4,5-T in the hamster.

Preliminary studies at FDA with 2,4-D in this species. A commercial sample of 2,4-D from a current plant production and one from a 1964 production from the same plant were tested. No sample of 2,4-D contained tetrachlorodibenzo-p-dioxin.

Details of these experiments are shown in the attached tables (6–11). Included are some data on 2,4,5-T with varying dioxin content.

Testing of 2,4-D at higher doses to establish a dose-response relationship will follow. Esters of 2,4-D (are also used as herbicides and these) will be studied for teratogenic potential.

Thus far the tetrachloro-p-dioxin has been shown to be responsible for teratological anomalies in animals, but information on other dioxins which may also be harmful is lacking. A number of pure dioxins will be tested in hamsters for teratogenic potential.

In toxicological evaluations, it is desirable to test a pesticide in more than one species, and studies with 2,4-D in rats are underway.

Tolerances for residues of 2,4-D at 5 parts per million have been established in or on apples, citrus fruits, pears and quinces and for residues of 0.5 parts per million in or on the grain of, and at 20 parts per million in or on the forage of barley, oats, rye and wheat. Such residue tolerances do not allow the presence of dioxins. If dioxins were detected on any of these raw agricultural commodities, they would be in violation of the Food, Drug, and Cosmetic Act and subject to seizure and/or other legal condemnation.

The pesticide surveillance activities of FDA are continuously examining food products for the chlorophenoxyacid class of herbicides. This surveillance effort has shown a very low level of 2,4,5-D residues in marketed food products. The "trace" analytical result is most frequently reported, corresponding to a level attributable to 2,4-D of less than 0.01 parts per million.

Mr. Chairman, I have in a very brief fashion outlined our investigations involving the chlorophenoxy herbicides, the chlorophenols and the dioxins. I believe we are moving very rapidly in this area. Severe restrictions were placed on the use of 2,4,5-T because of the hazard, particularly to women of childbearing ages, that could result from exposures to residues of 2,4,5-T. We are now continuing our investigations of 2,4,5-T and of the dioxins and of the chlorophenols. We are investigating 2,4-D very actively to determine if a hazard from it exists. We believe it imperative that our considerations of national policy for dealing with the questions posed by these herbicides take account of the tremendous benefit our society receives from the use of herbicides to produce an abundant and nutritious food supply. In view of the complexity of the issues together with the limitations of our ability to assess potential hazards to human health, it is essential that we respond wisely and not resort to extreme measures which the evidence does not warrant. The evidence that is available now does not in my judgment support a conclusion that formulations of 2,4-D as now marketed and under current uses present a hazard to the public health. Should our, or other evidence lead us to conclude that a hazard does exist, we shall take prompt and appropriate action to protect the public health.

TABLE 6 RESULTS OF TERATOLOGY STUDY WITH HAMSTERS—5/5/70

Compound	Amt. Injected Day 6–10	Feti Litter	Total # Fetus	# Alive	# Dead	Average Weight	Terata
Control	(6)	11.5	69	68	1–1 ED	1.87	—
Dow Sample from Dr. Courtney (no detectable dioxin)	100 mg/kg/day (6)	10.7	64	44[1]	20–19 ED, 1 LD	1.61	5/44–11.4%[2]
Dow #120110 (.07 ppm dioxin)	100 mg/kg/day (6)	11.3	68	36[3]	32–31 ED, 1 LD	1.64	—
Hercules X-17394 (no detectable dioxin)	100 mg/kg/day (5)	12.0	60	42[4]	18–15 ED, 3 LD	1.62	—
Monsanto NL-07-020 (2.9 ppm dioxin)	100 mg/kg/day (6)	14.5	87	77[5]	10–8 ED, 2 LD	1.70	4/77–5.19%[6]

[1] Two were abnormally pale and three showed gastric and intestinal hemorrhages.
[2] Absence of eyelid (2), one exencephaly, two incomplete fusion of skull.
[3] Two were abnormally pale.
[4] Three were abnormally pale, seven showed evidence of gastric and/or intestinal hemorrhages.
[5] Twelve were abnormally pale, ten showed evidence of gastric and/or intestinal hemorrhages.
[6] Terata included two with eye abnormalities, one cleft palate, and one with ectopia heart.
ED—Early Dead, LD—Late Dead.
Food and Drug Administration, Division of Pesticide Chemistry & Toxicology, Residue Toxicology Branch

TABLE 7 RESULTS OF TERATOLOGY STUDY WITH HAMSTERS—5/8/70

Compound	Amt. Injected Day 6–10	Feti Litter	Total # Fetus	# Alive	# Dead	Average Weight	Terata
Control	(6)	12.2	73	72	1–1 ED	1.72	—
2,4,5-T Dow (5 ppm dioxin)	100 mg/kg/day (6)	12.8	77	45[1]	32–31 ED, 1 LD	1.46	3/45–6.7%[2]
2,4,5-T Dow (5 ppm dioxin)	80 mg/kg/day (4)	9.3	37	28[3]	9–9 ED	1.53	1/28–3.6%[4]
2,4,5-T Dow (5 ppm dioxin)	40 mg/kg/day (5)	13.4	67	65[5]	2–2 ED	1.57	—
2,4,5-T K&K (45 ppm dioxin)	80 mg/kg/day (6)	13.3	80	2	78–37 ED, 41 LD	1.70	2/2–100%[6]

[1] Four were abnormally pale and showed gastric and/or intestinal hemorrhages.
[2] One exencephaly, one incomplete fusion of skull, one cleft palate.
[3] One showed gastric and/or intestinal hemorrhages.
[4] One showed incomplete fusion of skull.
[5] One was abnormally pale.
[6] Terata included eye abnormalities, and incomplete fusion of skull.
ED—Early Dead, LD—Late Dead.
Food and Drug Administration, Division of Pesticide Chemistry & Toxicology, Residue Toxicology Branch

TABLE 8   RESULTS OF TERATOLOGY STUDY WITH HAMSTERS—5/12/70

Compound	Amt. Injected Day 6–10	Feti Litter	Total # Fetus	# Alive	# Dead	Average Weight	Terata
Control	(5)	12.8	64	63	1–1 ED	1.85	—
2,4,5-T K&K (45 ppm dioxin)	100 mg/kg/day (5)	12.2	61	—	61–14 ED, 47 LD	—	—
2,4,5-T K&K (45 ppm dioxin)	40 mg/kg/day (5)	13.3	66	17[1]	49–14 ED, 35 LD	1.92	2/17–11.8%[2]
2,4,5-T Dow (.5 ppm dioxin)	80 mg/kg/day (4)	14.3	57	25[3]	32–31 ED, 1 LD	1.61	1/25–4.0%[4]
2,4,5-T Dow (.5 ppm dioxin)	40 mg/kg/day (4)	14.8	59	56[5]	3–2 ED, 1 LD	1.62	1/56–1.8%[6]

[1] Eight showed gastric and/or intestinal hemorrhages.
[2] Absence of eyelid.
[3] Three showed gastric and/or intestinal hemorrhages.
[4] Skull incompletely covered.
[5] Three showed gastric and/or intestinal hemorrhages, two were abnormally pale.
[6] Terata included exencephaly with spina bifida.
ED—Early Dead, LD—Late Dead.

Food and Drug Administration, Division of Pesticide Chemistry & Toxicology, Residue Toxicology Branch

TABLE 9 RESULTS OF TERATOLOGY STUDY WITH HAMSTERS—5/15/70

Compound	Amt. Injected Day 6–10	Feti Litter	Total # Fetus	# Alive	# Dead	Average Weight (g)	Terata
Control	(6)	11.2	67	65	2–2 ED	1.90	—
2,4-D Dow (Hansen) 1964 production	100 mg/kg/day (5)	10.6	53	45[1]	8–8 ED	1.44	1/45–2.2%
2,4-D Dow (Hansen)	40 mg/kg/day (5)	10.0	50	48[3]	2–2 ED	1.69	—
2,4,5-T Glasgow 69-144 Org. from Eastman	80 mg/kg/day (6)	11.8	71	46[4]	25–24 ED 1 LD	1.58	—
2,4,5-T Glasgow 69-144 Org. from Eastman	40 mg/kg/day (6)	11.0	66	55[5]	11–7 ED 4 LD	1.53	—

[1] Six of 45 alive appeared pale.
[2] Ear abnormality plus hemorrhage.
[3] One appeared pale in color.
[4] Four showed evidence of gastric and/or intestinal hemorrhages.
[5] Two showed evidence of gastric and/or intestinal hemorrhages.
ED—Early Dead, LD—Late Dead.
Food and Drug Administration, Division of Pesticide Chemistry & Toxicology, Residue Toxicology Branch

TABLE 10 RESULTS OF TERATOLOGY STUDY WITH HAMSTERS—5/22/70

Compound	Amt. Injected Day 6–10	Feti Litter	Total # Fetus	# Alive	# Dead	Average Weight (g)	Terata
Control	(4)	14.0	56	54	2–2 ED	1.86	—
2,4-D Dow (Hansen) 1964	40 mg/kg/day (6)	13.5	81	71[1]	10–5 ED 5 LD	1.78	—
2,4-D Dow F-719 current production	100 mg/kg/day (5)	15.8	79	74[2]	5–1 LD 4 ED	1.71	—
2,4,5-T Dow (5 ppm dioxin)	20 mg/kg/day (11)	13.8	154	140[3]	13–2 LD 11 ED	1.71	—

[1] One appeared pale.
[2] Five had apparent gastro-intestinal hemorrhages; several appeared pale.
[3] Twelve had apparent gastro-intestinal hemorrhages; one appeared pale.
ED—Early Dead, LD—Late Dead.
Food and Drug Administration, Division of Pesticide Chemistry & Toxicology, Residue Toxicology Branch

TABLE 11 RESULTS OF TERATOLOGY STUDY WITH HAMSTERS—5/19/70

Compound	Amt. Injected Day 6–10	Feti Litter	Total # Fetus	# Alive	# Dead	Average Weight (g)	Terata
Control	(5)	9.4	47	46	1–1 ED	1.89	—
2,4,5-T Purified Glasgow, 69-144 Eastman	100 mg/kg/day (6)	12.0	72	44[1]	28–28 ED	1.55	4/44–9.1%[2]
2,4,5-T K&K (45 ppm dioxin)	20 mg/kg/day (12)	10.8	130	88[3]	42–21 LD 21 ED	1.64	3/88–4.4%[4]
2,4-D Dow (Hansen) 1964	100 mg/kg/day (5)	11.4	57	53[5]	4–4 ED	1.82	—

[1] One had a hemorrhage in the spinal region.
[2] Poor fusion in head.
[3] 25 appeared to have gastric and/or intestinal hemorrhages.
[4] Poor fusion in head.
[5] Twelve appeared pale.
ED—Early Dead, LD—Late Dead.
Food and Drug Administration, Division of Pesticide Chemistry & Toxicology, Residue Toxicology Branch

Index

(Numbered chemicals such as 2,4-D and 2,4,5-T appear at the end of the index under *Numbered Chemicals.*)